FAVORITEN
PRESSE

ISBN 978-3-96849-058-8

Favoritenpresse, 2022
Die Favoritenpresse ist ein Imprint der
Verlagsagentur Bodo von Hodenberg
www.vonhodenberg.net

© 2013 by Luci Gutiérrez
The German edition is published by arrangement with
Luci Gutiérrez c/o MB Agencia Literaria S.L. through
Anoukh Foerg Literarische Agentur

Einleitung aus dem Englischen übersetzt von Eric Aichinger

Druck vermittelt durch Couleurs Print & More GmbH
www.couleurs-print.com

Informationen zum Verlagsprogramm:
www.favoritenpresse.de

ENGLISCH IST NICHT EASY

by LUCI GUTIÉRREZ

E s gibt zwei Arten von Menschen: jene, denen das Sprachenlernen leicht fällt und solche, die damit zu kämpfen haben. Ich gehöre zu letzteren. Sie vielleicht auch? Ich mag gar nicht daran denken, wieviele Stunden (und Geld!) ich für meine Anstrengungen, Englisch zu lernen, aufgewendet habe, während ich eigentlich jede einzelne Minute davon hasste. Weil die Leute ja aber ach so smart rüberkommen, wenn sie Englisch sprechen können, bin ich drangeblieben. Ich nahm an Online-Lehrgängen teil, machte Sommer-Intensivkurse. Sogar nach New York bin ich gereist, wo ich dann an bitterkalten Wintermorgen in aller Herrgottsfrühe in irgendein russisches Viertel in Brooklyn fuhr, das mir wie der Wilde Westen vorkam. In Sprachkursen am Times Square, die von irgendwelchen Lehrern mit höchst zweifelhaftem Akzent gegeben und die während des Unterrichts von besonders treu ergebenen japanischen Studentinnen massiert wurden, konnte ich meine Augen kaum aufhalten. Jede dieser Erfahrungen wurde selbstredend auch von einem Unterrichtsbuch begleitet, das so irrsinnig spannende Themen wie Extremsportarten und außergewöhnliche Witterungsverhältnisse behandelte. Sie wissen schon – das Alltagsvokabular, das man dringend benötigt, wenn man vor die Tür tritt und sieht, wie gerade ein Gleitschirmflieger von einem Hurrikan davongetragen wird.

All das hinter mich gebracht, musste ich – nun zurück auf der anderen Seite des Atlantiks – einen Weg finden, das Gelernte trotz meines furchtbaren Gedächtnisses irgendwie zu behalten. Und so kam ich dann darauf, dass meine Zeichenkünste mir beim Einprägen von Vokabeln und Grammatikregeln helfen würden. Aus diesen Zeichnungen ist schließlich das vorliegende Buch entstanden, und das Englischlernen wurde letztlich doch noch zum Vergnügen. Vielleicht funktioniert es bei Ihnen nicht – mir jedenfalls hat das Anfertigen der Zeichnungen für dieses Buch sehr dabei geholfen, wenigstens ein paar englische Worte sinnvoll aneinanderreihen zu können. Und – komme nicht auch ich jetzt ach so smart rüber?

lesson 1

THE
ENGLISH ALPHABET

A   A [eɪ]   B   BEE [biː]   C   CEE [siː]   D   DEE [diː]   E   E [iː]

F   EF [ɛf]   G   GEE [dʒiː]   H   AITCH [eɪtʃ]   I   i [ai]   J   JAY [dʒeɪ]   K   KAY [keɪ]

L   EL [ɛl]   M   EM [ɛm]   N   EN [ɛn]   O   0 [ou]   P   PEE [piː]

Q   CUE [kjuː]   R   AR [ar]   S   ESS [ɛs]   T   TEE [tiː]   U   U [juː]

V   VEE [viː]   W   DOUBLE-U [ˈdʌbəlju]   X   EX [ɛks]   Y   WY [waɪ]   Z   ZEE [zē]

SUBJECT
P R O N O U N S

PERSON		PRONOUN
singular	1st	*I*
	2nd	*You*
	3rd male	*He*
	3rd female	*She*
	3rd neutral	*It*
plural	1st	*We*
	2nd	*You*
	3rd	*They*

Subject pronouns indicate the person or object we are talking about.

Third person singular, neutral.

First person singular.

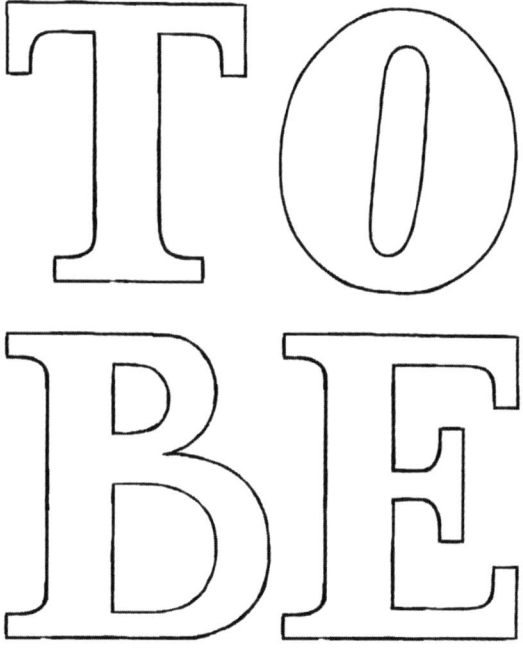

The verb "to be" means to exist.

to be
in the
Present
Simple

The
SIMPLE PRESENT FORM
of TO BE.

I am | I'm
You are | You're
He is | He's
She is | She's
It is | It's
We are | We're
You are | You're
They are | They're

To make
NEGATIVES,
insert NOT after the verb "to be".

I am not | I'm not
You are not | You aren't
He is not | He isn't
She is not | She isn't
It is not | It isn't
We are not | We aren't
You are not | You aren't
They are not | They aren't

To make
QUESTIONS,
invert the subject and the verb.

Am I ... ?
Are you ... ?
Is he ... ?
Is she ... ?
Is it ... ?
Are we ... ?
Are you ... ?
Are they ... ?

Place PREPOSITIONS

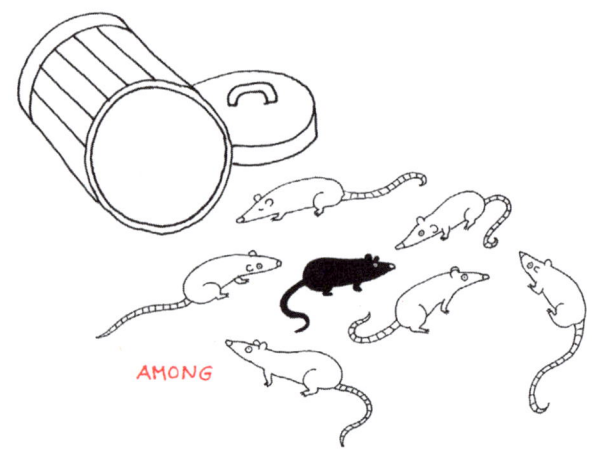

AMONG

ON

OVER

IN FRONT OF

IN

UNDER

BEHIND

NEXT TO

BETWEEN

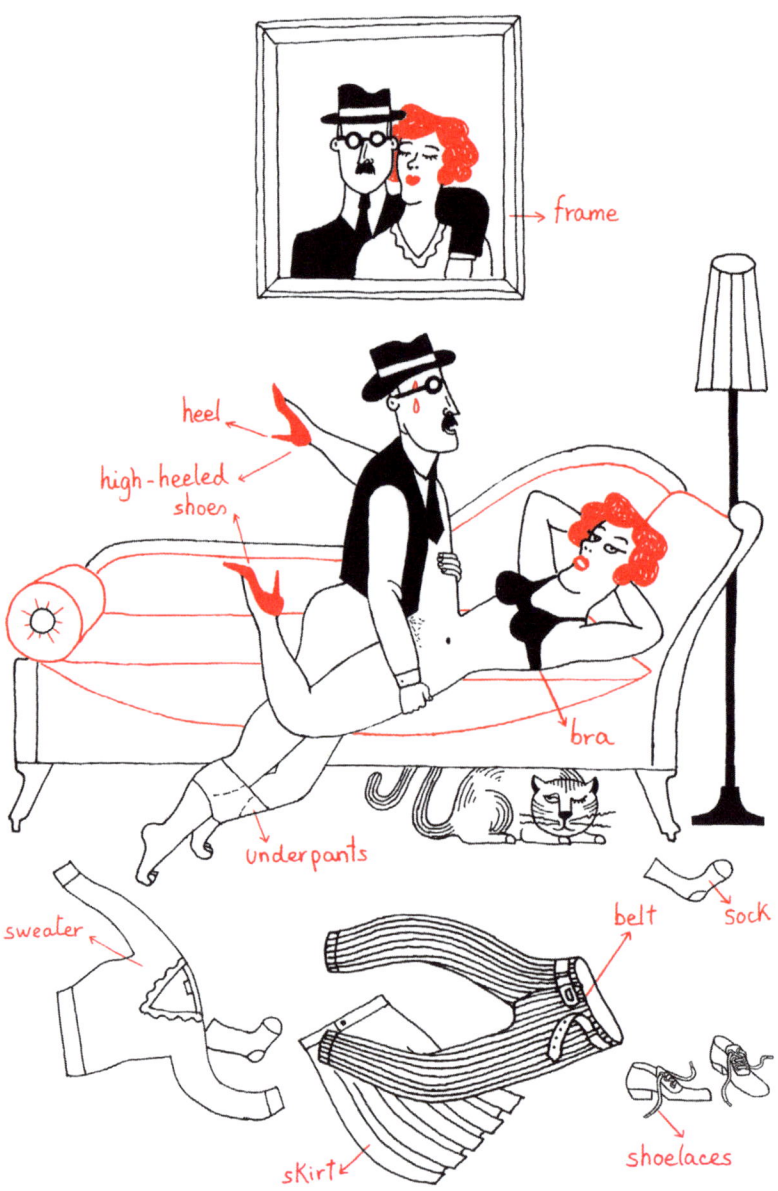

frame

heel

high-heeled shoes

bra

underpants

sweater

skirt

belt

sock

shoelaces

Where Is It?

The lamp is <u>next to</u> the chaise lounge.

The cat is <u>under</u> the chaise lounge.

The pants are <u>in front of</u> the cat.

The picture is <u>behind</u> the chaise lounge.

Mr. Sweat is <u>in</u> Mrs. Sweat.

WHERE ARE THESE PEOPLE FROM ?

QUESTION
Words

Where is he
from ?

Who is he ?

What's his
address ?

What's his
name ?

What's his
phone number ?

How much
does he earn ?

What does
he do ?

What's he
like ?

What is
he into ?

How old
is he ?

QUESTION WORDS are used
to ask for information and require more than a "yes" or "no" answer.

QUESTION WORD	ASKING FOR
WHAT	information about something *What's his name?*
WHEN	time *When is he coming?*
WHERE	place *Where is he from?*
WHO	person *Who is he?*
WHY	reason *Why do you like him?*
HOW	manner *How is he in bed?*
WHICH	choice *Which one do you like?*
WHOSE	possession *Whose bag is this?*
WHOM	which person *Whom are you going to date?*
HOW MUCH | HOW MANY	quantity *How much does he earn?*
HOW COME	reason (informal expression for "why?") *How come he doesn't call me?*

If the question word is the object of the **PREPOSITION**, put the preposition at the end.
Where is he <u>from</u>? or *What did he come <u>for</u>?*

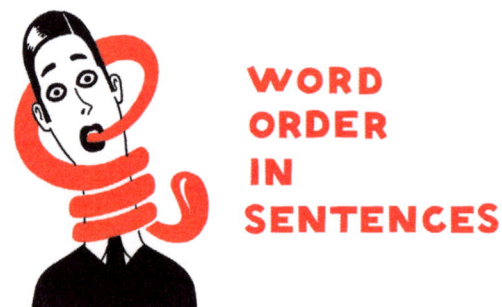

WORD ORDER IN SENTENCES

positive SENTENCES

SUBJECT	+ VERB	+ INDIRECT OBJECT	+ DIRECT OBJECT	+ PLACE	+ TIME
They	*will give*	*you*	*a terrible beating*	*at school*	*tomorrow.*
I	*wish*	*you*	*the best.*		

questions

QUESTION WORD +	AUXILIARY VERB +	SUBJECT	+ VERB	INDIRECT OBJECT
Why	*did*	*you*	*send*	*him*
Where	*were*	*you*	*—*	*—*

negative SENTENCES

SUBJECT	+ VERB	+ INDIRECT OBJECT	+ DIRECT OBJECT	+ PLACE	+ TIME
She	*didn't tell*	*him*	*the truth*	*at the pub*	*yesterday.*
He	*won't trust*	*her*	*—*	*—*	*anymore.*

Same as positive sentences, but negative sentences need an auxiliary verb and "not"
(except for the verb "to be").

+ DIRECT OBJECT	+ PLACE	+ TIME
anonymous letters	*to his office*	*every day?*
—	*—*	*the night of the murder?*

In questions, the auxiliary verb (or the main verb "to be") goes before the subject and
interrogatives go at the beginning of the sentence.

lesson

2

SIMPLE PRESENT

SUBJECT + VERB
You need...

YOU NEED a boyfriend that SAYS to you 'I LOVE YOU, baby'

The **SIMPLE PRESENT** is used to make statements about the present time.
For permanent facts that are always true: *The night is dark.*
For present facts that are true now: *I feel happy.*
For habitual actions: *I get up late.*

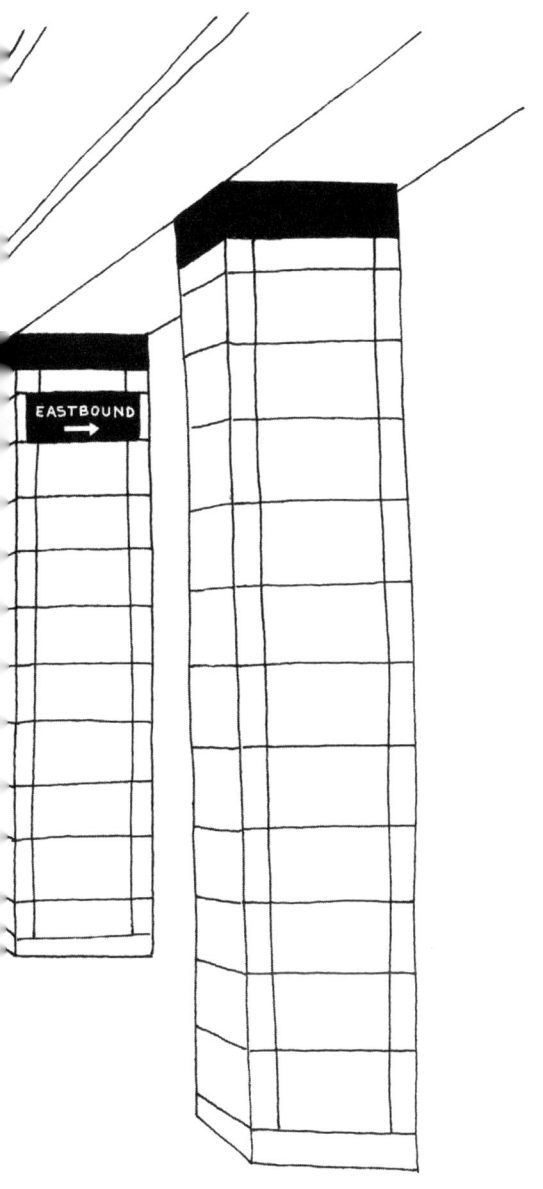

EASTBOUND
→

The **SIMPLE PRESENT**
is also used to talk about
scheduled events in the near future,
for example, when talking about events
that happen at a set time like timetables,
meetings or programs.

The train <u>arrives</u> at 1 a.m.
The meeting <u>begins</u> after lunch.
The show <u>ends</u> in five minutes.

NEGATIVE

To make a Simple Present negative use:
SUBJECT + DON'T | DOESN'T + INFINITIVE without "to"
I don't like...

DO + NOT = DON'T | DOES + NOT = DOESN'T

I DON'T LIKE PEOPLE.

QUESTION

To make a Simple Present question use:
DO | DOES + SUBJECT + INFINITIVE without "to"
Do you read?

In **SIMPLE PRESENT,**
add S to the verb in the third person singular (he, she, it).

I look great.
You look great.
He looks great.
She looks great.
It looks great.
We look great.
You look great.
They look great.

For verbs ending in O add ES: *do - does.*
For verbs ending in S add ES: *kiss - kisses.*
For verbs ending in X add ES: *mix - mixes.*
For verbs ending in CH add ES: *catch - catches.*
For verbs ending in SH add ES: *push - pushes.*
For verbs ending in Y after a consonant change Y to IES: *cry - cries.*

Use "doesn't" to form **NEGATIVES** and "does" for **QUESTIONS**.

I don't snore.	Do I stink?
You don't snore.	Do you stink?
He doesn't snore.	Does he stink?
She doesn't snore.	Does she stink?
It doesn't snore.	Does it stink?
We don't snore.	Do we stink?
You don't snore.	Do you stink?
They don't snore.	Do they stink?

PLURALS

When a countable noun refers to two or more things,
use the plural form of the noun.

Plurals are generally created
by **ADDING S** to the noun.

computer - computers

phantom - phantoms

umbrella - umbrellas

house - houses

book - books

hat - hats

With some nouns it is a little different.
These are the most **COMMON EXCEPTIONS**.

FOR NOUNS ENDING IN:

O, S, X, ZZ, CH, SH, add ES:

potato - potatoes
kiss - kisses
box - boxes
buzz - buzzes
witch - witches
dish - dishes

For a noun ending in **Z**, add ZES.
quiz - quizzes
And for some nouns ending in **O**, add S.
photo - photos
piano - pianos

CONSONANT + Y, change Y to IES.
city - cities

MOST NOUNS ENDING IN F OR FE, change to VES.
wolf - wolves

MOST NOUNS ENDING IN IS, change to ES.
crisis - crises

WOMAN   WOMEN

IRREGULAR PLURALS

IRREGULAR NOUNS
don't follow the previous rules.
These are the most common.

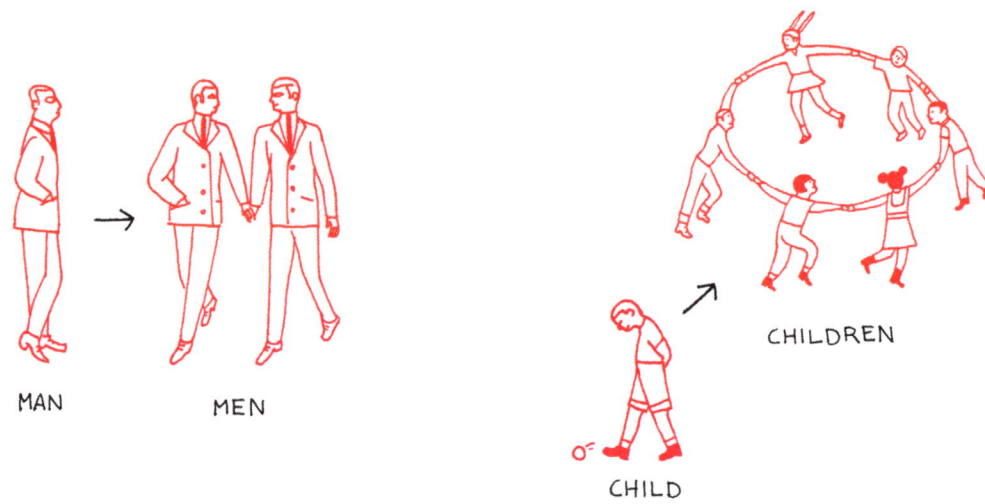

MAN   MEN

CHILDREN

CHILD

FOOT → FEET

SHEEP → SHEEP

TOOTH → TEETH

PERSON → PEOPLE

MOUSE → MICE

COUNTABLE
AND
UNCOUNTABLE
NOUNS

A **COUNTABLE NOUN**
can have a number in front of it
and can be plural:
3 years, 2 suitcases, 1 rabbit

An **UNCOUNTABLE NOUN**
cannot have a number in front of it
and there is no plural form:
air, water, oil, hope

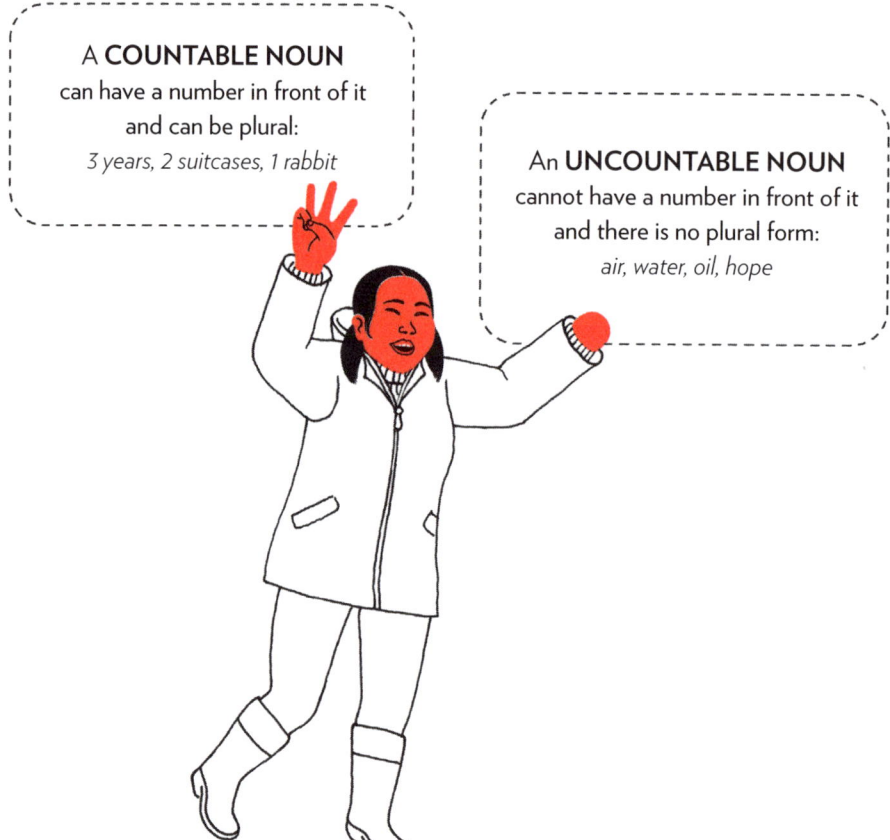

ARTICLES
WITH
COUNTABLE
AND
UNCOUNTABLE
NOUNS

A | AN, THE

Use a **COUNTABLE NOUN:**

with **A | AN**
the first time you use that noun.
There is a naked man in the garden.

A- when the noun starts with consonant: *a friend*
AN- when the noun starts with vowel: *an egg*

with **THE**
the subsequent times you use the noun, or
when the listener already knows what you
are referring to.
The naked man is dancing.

Use a **PLURAL COUNTABLE NOUN:**
with **NO ARTICLE**
when you speak in general.
I don't like children.

Use an **UNCOUNTABLE NOUN:**

with **NO ARTICLE**
if you mean all or any of that thing.
I don't need help.

with **THE**
when you are talking about
a particular example.
Thanks for the help you didn't give me before.

HOW MUCH | HOW MANY

Use "how much?"
to ask about something that is
UNCOUNTABLE.

Use "how many?"
to ask about something that is
COUNTABLE.

~~1 money~~
~~2 money~~
~~3 moneys~~

1 orange
2 oranges
3 oranges

SOME and ANY
are used when the speaker doesn't specify a number or an exact amount.

SOME is used in **POSITIVE SENTENCES**
with uncountable nouns:
You have _some butter_ on your nose.
with plural countable nouns:
You have _some boogers_ in your nose.

ANY is used in **NEGATIVE SENTENCES** and **QUESTIONS**
with uncountable nouns:
I don't want _any risk_ in my life.
with plural countable nouns:
Do you have _any friends_?

Two common exceptions to these rules:

Use **SOME** in questions when offering | requesting:
Would you like _some more tea_, darling?

Use **ANY** in positive sentences when it means "it doesn't matter which":
You can call me _at any time_.

"There is" and "there are" are used to say that something exists or doesn't exist.

THERE IS is used for a singular subject.

THERE ARE is used for a plural subject.

There is an ice rink.

There are a lot of buildings.

There are no trees.

There is no King Kong.

Are there any school buses?

Yes, *there are.*

Are there people skating?

Yes, *there is* a guy skating on an ice rink

and *there is* a girl skating on a building.

Is there a businessman in a hurry?

No, *there isn't.*

Demonstratives
THiS · THESE · THAT · THOSE

Demonstratives are used to show the distance from the speaker.
The distance can be psychological or physical.

THIS: for singular nouns that are near.
THESE: for plural nouns that are near.
THAT: for singular nouns that are far.
THOSE: for plural nouns that are far.

THiS   THESE

near

Demonstratives can be:

PRONOUNS	ADJECTIVES
This is the dead tree.	_This_ tree is dead.
I don't like _that_.	I came in _that_ car.
These are mine.	I left _these_ garbage bags.
Those are my neighbors.	_Those_ guys are unpleasant.

THAT   **THOSE**

- - - - - - - - - - - - - - - - - ▶ far

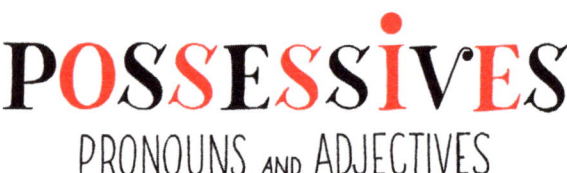

POSSESSIVES
PRONOUNS AND ADJECTIVES

SUBJECT PRONOUN	POSSESSIVE PRONOUN	POSSESSIVE ADJECTIVE
I	**MINE**	**MY**
You	**YOURS**	**YOUR**
He	**HIS**	**HIS**
She	**HERS**	**HER**
It	**ITS**	**ITS**
We	**OURS**	**OUR**
You	**YOURS**	**YOUR**
They	**THEIRS**	**THEIR**

POSSESSIVE PRONOUNS
are used instead of a noun.
Peggy's dress is pink. <u>Mine</u> is black.

POSSESSIVE ADJECTIVES
are usually used to describe a noun, and, like other adjectives, come before the noun.
<u>My</u> dress is nicer than <u>her</u> dress.

VIVIAN'S HUSBAND IS
EVERY WOMAN'S DREAM HUSBAND.

+ NOUNS

Use a **SINGULAR NOUN** with **'S** to show possession:
I don't like <u>my sister's boyfriend</u>.

Use **'S** with a **REGULAR PLURAL NOUN**:
I love <u>ladies' shoes</u>.
or an **IRREGULAR PLURAL NOUN**:
I don't care about <u>men's shoes</u>.

With **NAMES**:
<u>Kate's dog</u> barks every night.
Do you have <u>Susan's phone number</u>?

When a name ends in **S**, treat it like any other singular noun and add **'S**.
Don't eat <u>Charles's breakfast</u>.

lesson 3

VOCABULARY:
The Body and Stuff

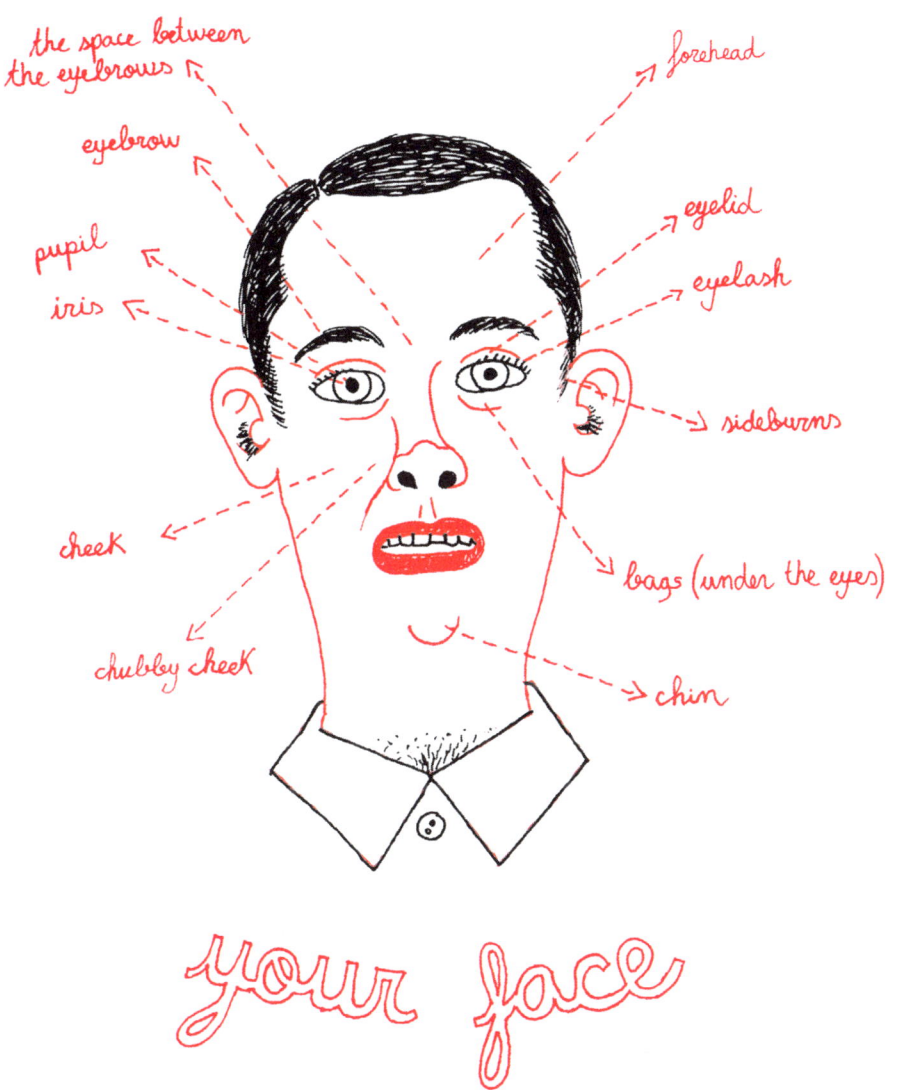

the space between
the eyebrows

forehead

eyebrow

eyelid

pupil

eyelash

iris

sideburns

cheek

bags (under the eyes)

chubby cheek

chin

your face

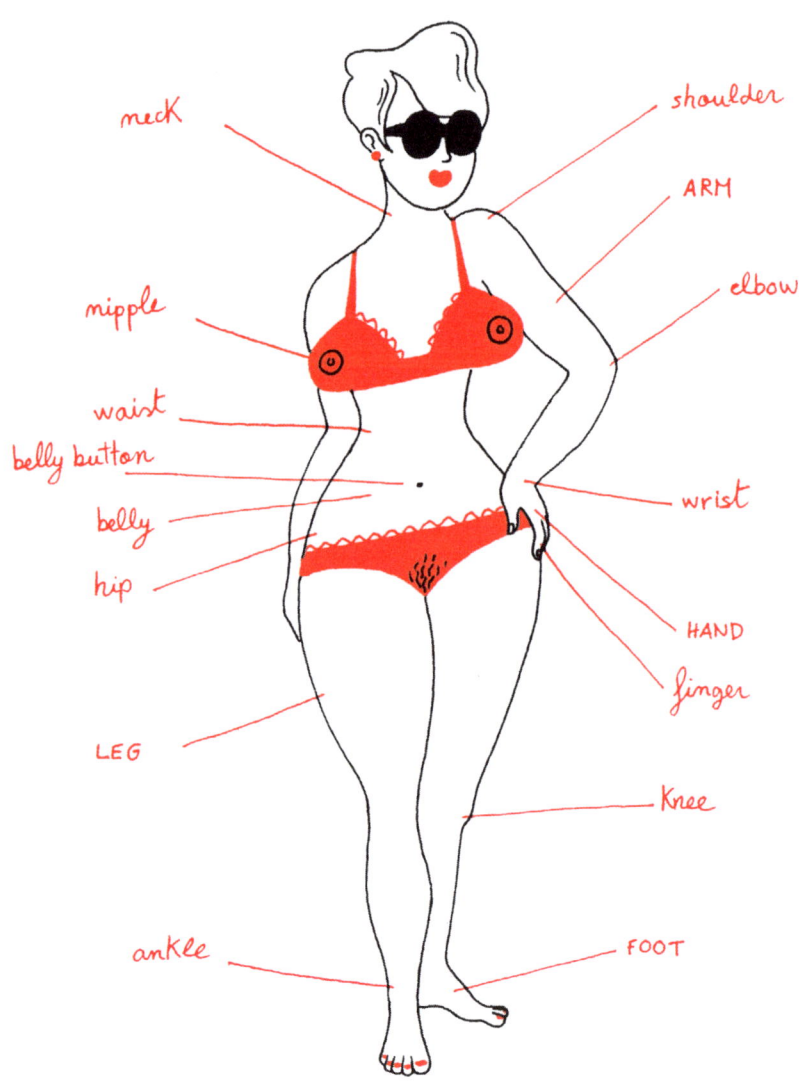

neck

shoulder

ARM

elbow

nipple

waist

belly button

belly

hip

wrist

HAND

finger

LEG

Knee

ankle

FOOT

You can see her BOOBS and her LADY PARTS! SHAMELESS!!!

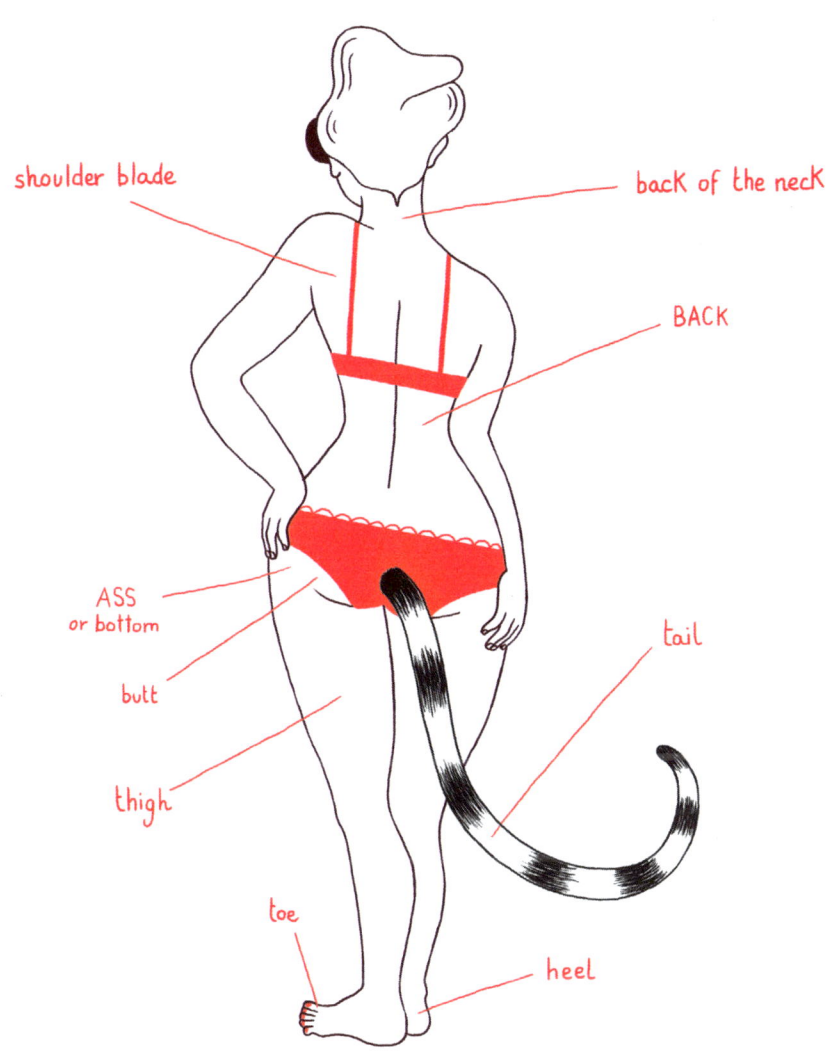

shoulder blade

back of the neck

BACK

ASS
or bottom

butt

tail

thigh

toe

heel

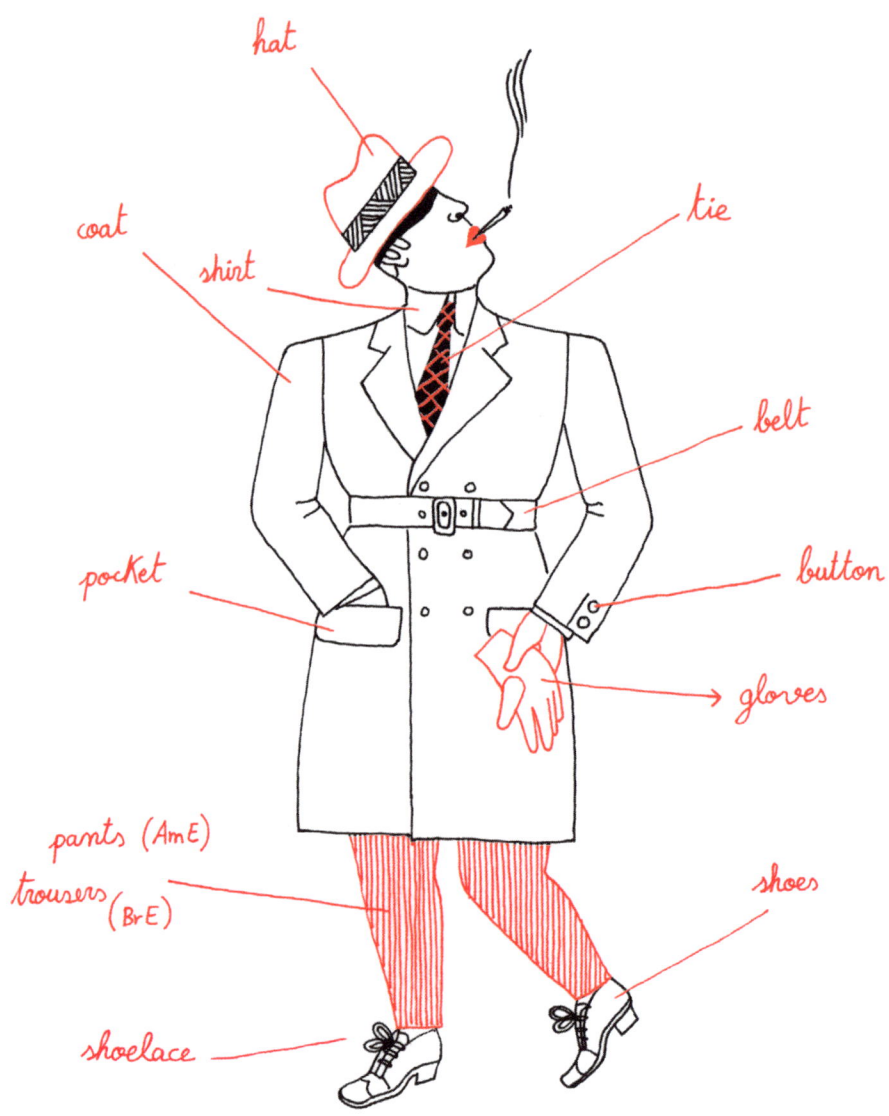

hat

coat

shirt

tie

belt

button

pocket

gloves

pants (AmE)
trousers (BrE)

shoes

shoelace

VOCABULARY *for an elegant man*

VOCABULARY
for a MAN'S BODY

is the same as
for a woman's body,
but with a few differences.
Here they are:

Men don't have boobs.
They only have a
CHEST

But they have
NIPPLES

CHEST HAIR
This is especially for
macho men, but some
women can have it, too.

PENIS
also called:
cock
dick
phallus
or hot-dog

It has so many
names because
most men are very
proud of having
one.

TESTICLES
or
BALLS

It's plural because
there are two.

SOCKS

VOCABULARY *for the man's body*

The 5 Senses

You can get pleasure through the five senses
if you don't have any disability.

My sense of <u>smell</u> is almost non-existent.

I have refined <u>taste.</u>

His <u>touch</u> is unpleasant.

Speak up! My <u>hearing</u> is getting worse.

She fell in love at first <u>sight</u>.

JOBS

This is what we do to earn money.

Use the article **A | AN**
before a job.
I'm a waitress.

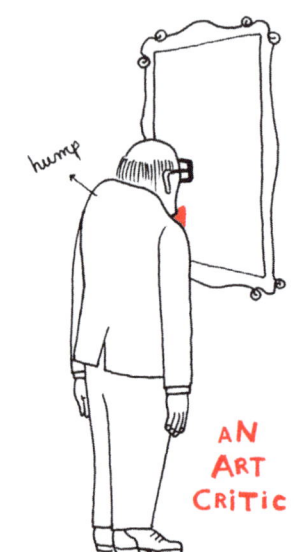

AN
ART
CRITIC

chocolate
strawberry
jam

A
PASTRY
CHEF

A HOTEL ATTENDANT

A PIANIST

A MOBSTER

cap

Wait outside!

A WAITRESS

A BUTCHER

sweet sausage

A HOMELESS PERSON

grandmother
granddaughter
mother-in-law
daugter-in-law
son
wife
brother
husband
wife
father
daughter
mother
sister

CARRIE

PHIL

ELISA

JOHN

SUE

MADELEINE

family

Carrie and Phil got married 24 years ago. John, their son, is 24 years old. Carrie and Phil usually say he was conceived on their wedding night, but the family knows it was before. Elisa is a rebellious teenager. She is 14 years old. She hates to spend time with her family. She wants to be different and, more than anything, she doesn't want to be like her mother. Elisa has a sister in law, Sue, who has brought a new baby into the family and the new tradition of barbecuing on Sundays. The grandparents are in love with little Madeleine, as is John, but there is something they don't know: John is not really her father. That's a little family secret.

How many siblings do you have?

I have 4 siblings.
I have 2 brothers
and 2 sisters.
But I would
prefer to
have
none.

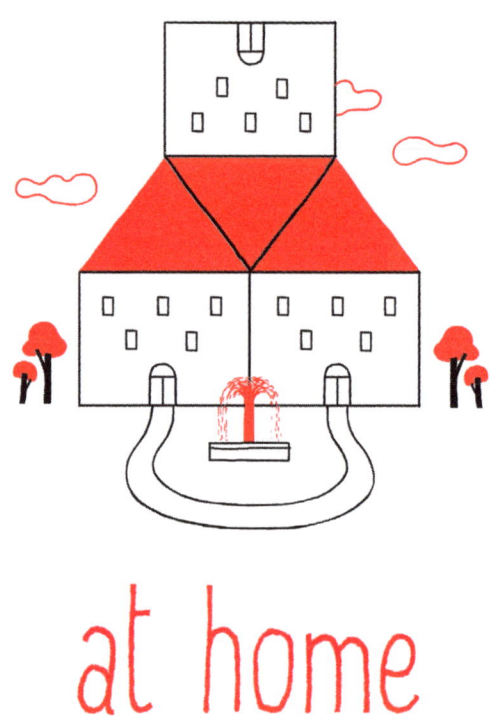

at home

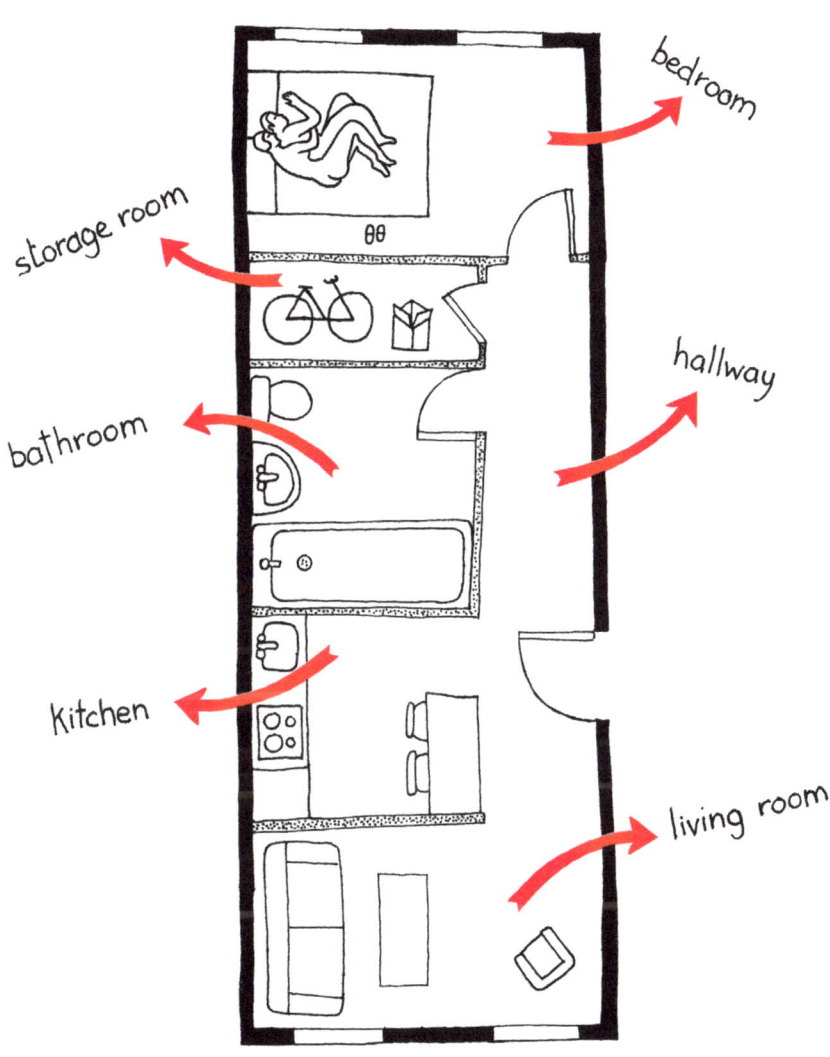

bedroom

storage room

hallway

bathroom

kitchen

living room

furniture

stool   chair   armchair   sofa or couch

lamp

bookshelf

table

carpet or rug

Let's Eat!

8A.M. Breakfast

12P.M. Lunch

ANY TIME! Snack

= MENU =

★ STARTERS ★

- APPETIZERS

- SOUPS

- SALADS

- SANDWICHES

- PASTA

★ MAIN COURSES ★

- FISH

- SEAFOOD

MEATS

CHICKEN

PORK

BEEF

- SIDE
DISHES

★ DESSERTS ★

★ BEVERAGES ★

WINES

SODAS

BEERS

french fries

burger

cheeseburger

chicken wings

pretzel

hot dog

sausage

FOOD Vocabulary

fried egg

noodles

omelet

chips

olive oil

pepperoni pizza

salt & pepper

ketchup & mustard

onion rings

sushi

bread

MashedPotatoes

mashed potatoes

cheese

loaf of bread

pickles

jam

marshmallows

cookie

butter

sugar

croissant

donut

SKIPPY

peanut butter

cheesecake

muffin

seafood

shrimp

mussels

vegetables

onion

parsley

peas

tomato

cucumber

asparagus

mushrooms

lettuce

eggplant

artichoke

garlic

carrot

green beans

red pepper

fruit

peach

watermelon

coconut

pear

pineapple

lemon

strawberry

melon

banana

peanuts

nuts

almonds

walnuts

hazelnuts

lesson

VOCABULARY
VERBS

TO WALK

TO JUMP

TO FLY

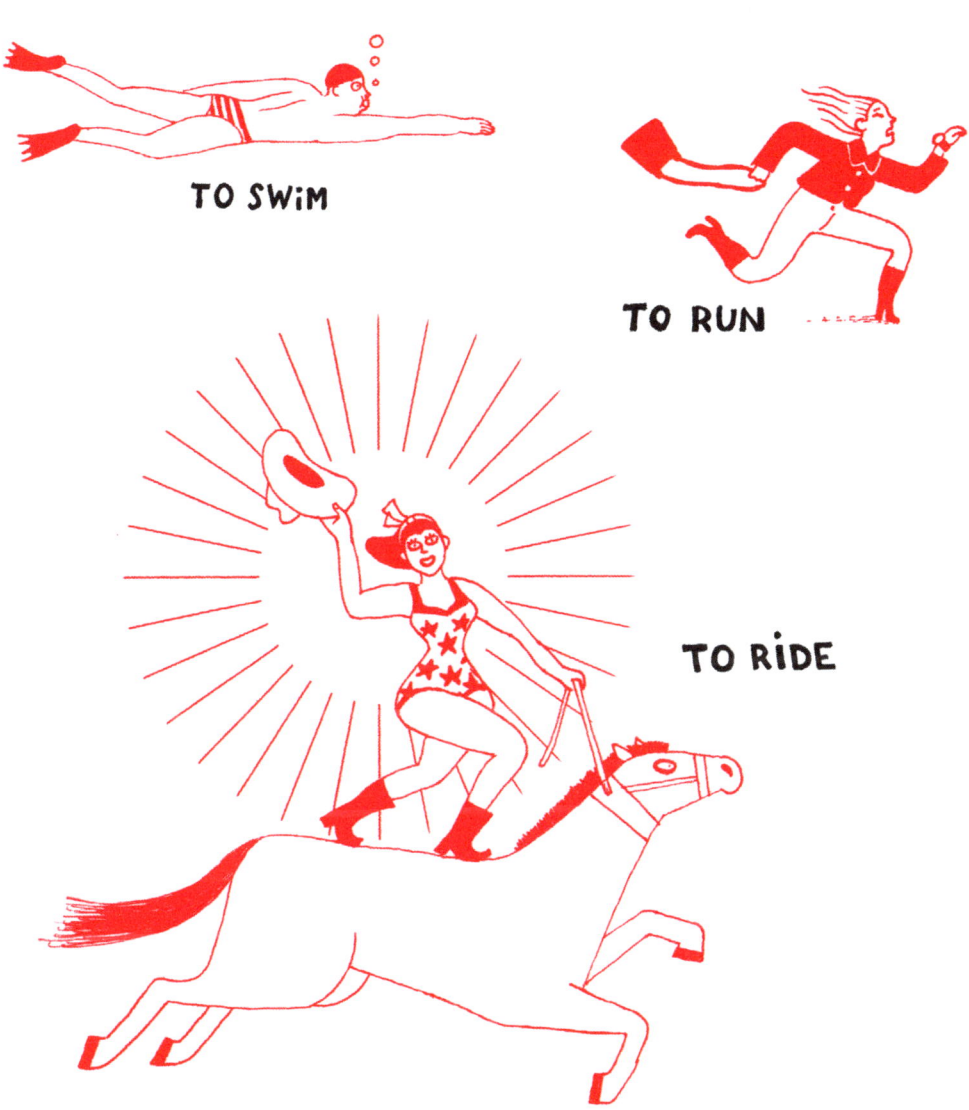

TO SWIM

TO RUN

TO RIDE

TO ARGUE

TO HUG

TO THROW

TO REST

TO REALIZE

The day after arguing with his wife, hugging her, getting dishes thrown at him and resting, Jeff realized he was wearing his slippers on the way back home from work.

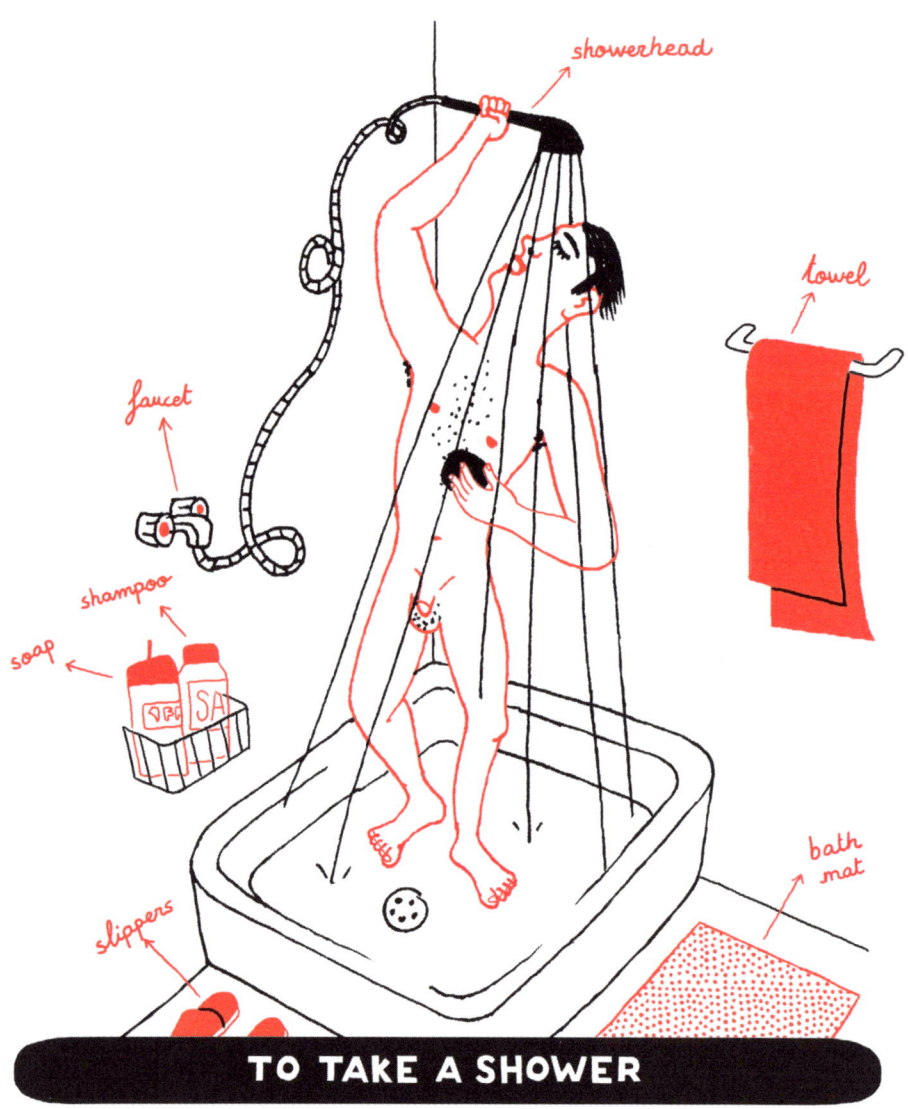

showerhead

towel

faucet

shampoo

soap

slippers

bath mat

TO TAKE A SHOWER

He <u>takes a shower</u> when he gets up, after the gym, after having sex and before going to bed.
Between showers, he works in an organization that fights global warming.

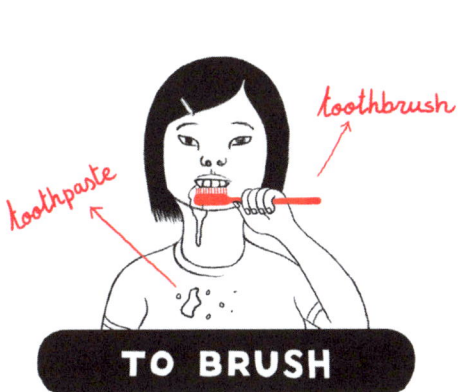

TO BRUSH

She is a little dirty. She gets dirty even when she <u>brushes</u> her teeth.

TO COMB

He usually <u>combs</u> his hair with gel because his lover likes it.

TO WEAR

He <u>wears</u> this hat and these glasses to feel like a more interesting person.

TO UNDO

She <u>is undoing</u> the buttons of her shirt to do a striptease for her gynecologist.

to
CHEW

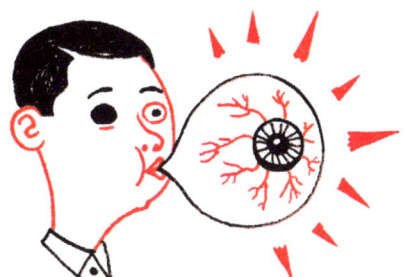

Tim was a sensitive and delicate boy. His classmates used to laugh at him. One day after school, Tim was shot by a slingshot*. He lost an eye. Ever since that day, Tim walks around school with a hole in his face, <u>chewing</u> and blowing what looks like his lost eye. Now, Tim is every kid's nightmare.

GET tired
= BECOME

GET the bus
= CATCH

GET

"To get" has a lot of meanings!

GET wet
= BECOME

GET help
= OBTAIN

GET the ball
= CATCH

GET home
= ARRIVE

$E=mc^2$

GET the lesson
= UNDERSTAND

GET a letter
= RECEIVE

GET groceries
= BUY

the IMPERATIVE

Use the verb **WITHOUT A PRONOUN**:

To give a **DIRECT ORDER**.
Take your hands off my legs.

On **SIGNS** and **NOTICES**.
Do not touch.

To give **INSTRUCTIONS**.
Carry on when you get to the edge.

To give **INFORMAL ADVICE**.
Tell him how much you hate him.

To **INVITE**.
Sit closer, please.

the F line poem

Take the F line to Brooklyn
if you are lucky, you'll arrive in the evening.
Let's go to Avenue N
where English class will never end.
Go past Avenue I
then Bay Parkway you'll see with your eyes.
Don't miss the cemetery from the train!
Next stop is Avenue N
but suddenly you are on Avenue P.
Isn't Avenue N where you should be?
The F line is unpredictable
from local to express service, it's quite variable.
Get back on the F line to Manhattan
if you don't want to take a walk on Coney Island.
So _wait_ for the next train on Avenue P
your frozen nose you will see.
Hey! Not so bad, the F train is coming
but again you miss Avenue N until tomorrow morning.

lesson

to be
in the Simple Past

The
SIMPLE PAST FORM
of TO BE.

I was
You were
He was
She was
It was
We were
You were
They were

To make **NEGATIVES**,
insert "not" after the conjugated
form of "to be".

I was not | I wasn't
You were not | You weren't
He was not | He wasn't
She was not | She wasn't
It was not | It wasn't
We were not | We weren't
You were not | You weren't
They were not | They weren't

To make **QUESTIONS**,
invert the subject
and the verb.

Was I ... ?
Were you ... ?
Was he ... ?
Was she ... ?
Was it ... ?
Were we ... ?
Were you ... ?
Were they ... ?

Simple Past

SUBJECT + PAST FORM

She lived...

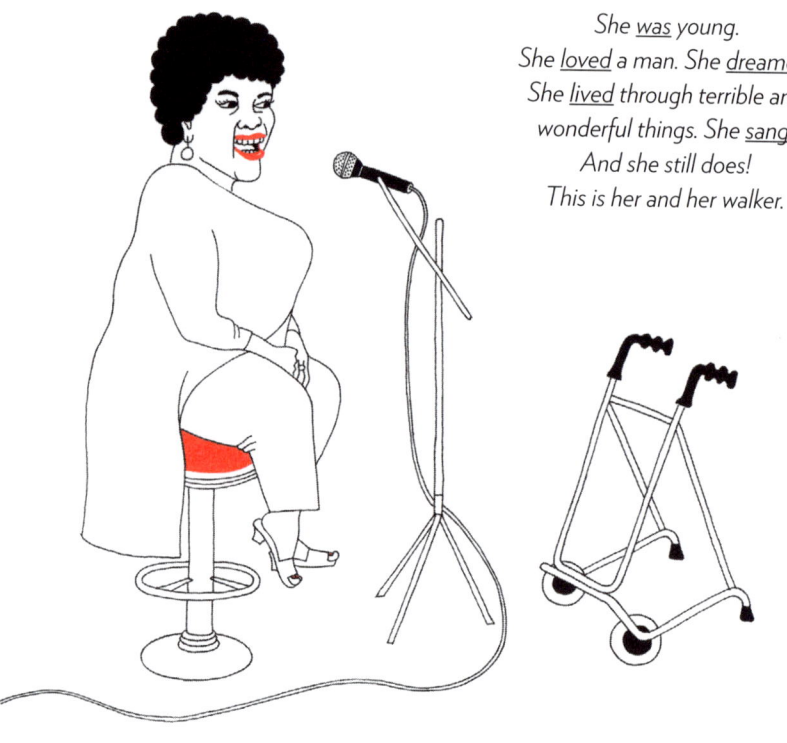

She <u>was</u> young.
She <u>loved</u> a man. She <u>dreamed.</u>
She <u>lived</u> through terrible and
wonderful things. She <u>sang</u>.
And she still does!
This is her and her walker.

The **SIMPLE PAST** describes an action or situation in the past.
When the event is in the past: *My childhood <u>was</u> happy.*
When the event is completely finished: *I <u>washed</u> all the dishes.*
When we say (or understand) the time | place of the event: *I <u>woke up</u> in Phil's bed.*

forming the simple past tense

With regular verbs,
the Simple Past is created simply by adding **ED**,
but with some verbs it is a little different.

FOR VERBS ENDING IN:

E, add D:
live - lived

CONSONANT+Y, change Y to I and add ED:
cry - cried

ONE VOWEL+ONE CONSONANT (but not W | Y),
double the consonant and add ED:
commit - committed

ANYTHING ELSE, add ED:
jump - jumped

negative

To make a Simple Past negative use:
SUBJECT + DID NOT | DIDN'T + INFINITIVE without "to"
I didn't go...

DID + NOT = DIDN'T

I **didn't go** to school today.

question

To make a Simple Past question use:
DID + SUBJECT + INFINITIVE without "to"
Did you love her?

There are many irregular verbs in English
that do not add ED in the past form.

infinitive	simple past	past participle	meaning
ARISE	AROSE	ARISEN	emerge
AWAKE	AWOKE	AWOKEN	stop sleeping
BE	WAS | WERE	BEEN	exist
BEAT	BEAT	BEATEN | BEAT	hit repeatedly
BECOME	BECAME	BECOME	begin to be
BEGIN	BEGAN	BEGUN	start
BEND	BENT	BENT	force sth. into a curve
BET	BET	BET	risk something
BITE	BIT	BITTEN	use the teeth to cut
BLEED	BLED	BLED	loose blood
BLOW	BLEW	BLOWN	exhale hard
BREAK	BROKE	BROKEN	separate into pieces
BRING	BROUGHT	BROUGHT	carry or convey

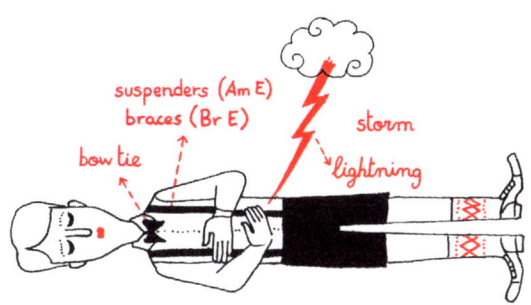

He has a heart but it doesn't <u>beat</u> anymore.

TO BURST
BURST – BURST – BURST

TO FEED
FEED FED FED

infinitive	simple past	past participle	meaning
BUILD	BUILT	BUILT	construct
BURN	BURNED | BURNT	BURNED | BURNT	be destroyed by fire
BURST	BURST	BURST	cause to break by puncture
BUY	BOUGHT	BOUGHT	obtain in exchange for payment
CATCH	CAUGHT	CAUGHT	intercept and hold
CHOOSE	CHOSEN	CHOSEN	select
CLING	CLUNG	CLUNG	hold on tightly
COME	CAME	COME	move toward the speaker
COST	COST	COST	have a price
CREEP	CREPT	CREPT	move slowly
CUT	CUT	CUT	make an incision
DEAL	DEALT	DEALT	distribute or sell
DIG	DUG	DUG	extract earth from the ground
DIVE	DIVED | DOVE	DIVED	plunge into water
DO	DID	DONE	make | perform
DRAW	DREW	DRAWN	make a picture with lines
DREAM	DREAMED | DREAMT	DREAMED | DREAMT	imagine during sleep
DRINK	DRANK	DRUNK	the act of swallowing a liquid
DRIVE	DROVE	DRIVEN	operate a motor vehicle
EAT	ATE	EATEN	ingest food
FALL	FELL	FALLEN	move downward without control
FEED	FED	FED	give food
FEEL	FELT	FELT	be aware of a physical sensation
FIGHT	FOUGHT	FOUGHT	take part in a struggle | argue
FIND	FOUND	FOUND	discover something

infinitive	past simple	past participle	meaning
FIT	FIT | FITTED	FIT	be the right size or shape
FLEE	FLED	FLED	run away
FLING	FLUNG	FLUNG	throw forcefully
FLY	FLEW	FLOWN	move through the air
FORBID	FORBADE | FORBID	FORBIDDEN	refuse to allow
FORGET	FORGOT	FORGOTTEN	cease remembering
FORGIVE	FORGAVE	FORGIVEN	stop feeling angry toward someone
FREEZE	FROZE	FROZEN	turn into ice
GET	GOT	GOTTEN | GOT	come to have | obtain | receive
GIVE	GAVE	GIVEN	transfer sth. to someone
GO	WENT	GONE	move from one place to another
GRIND	GROUND	GROUND	reduce to small pieces by crushing
GROW	GREW	GROWN	progress to maturity or in size
HANG	HUNG	HUNG	suspend
HAVE	HAD	HAD	possess, own or hold
HEAR	HEARD	HEARD	perceive sound
HIDE	HID	HIDDEN	put or keep out of sight
HIT	HIT	HIT	come into contact forcefully
HOLD	HELD	HELD	keep with one's arms or hands
HURT	HURT	HURT	cause physical pain
KEEP	KEPT	KEPT	have or retain possession of
KNEEL	KNELT | KNEELED	KNELT | KNEELED	support oneself on one's knees
KNIT	KNIT | KNITTED	KNIT | KNITTED	work wool with needles
KNOW	KNEW	KNOWN	perceive directly
LAY	LAID	LAID	put in position

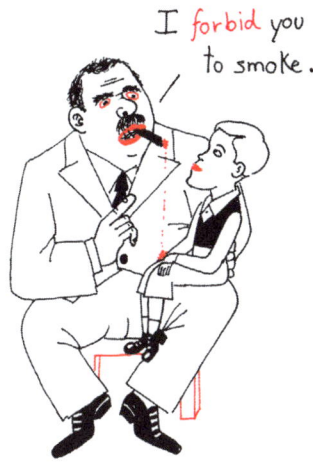

TO FORBID
FORBID-FORBADE-FORBIDDEN

Little Monkey hanged Thomas while he <u>hung</u> from a tree.

HANG HUNG HUNG
& HANG HANGED HANGED

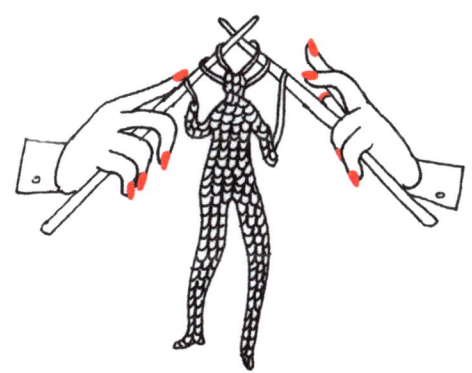

TO KNIT
KNIT-KNIT|KNITTED-KNIT|KNITTED

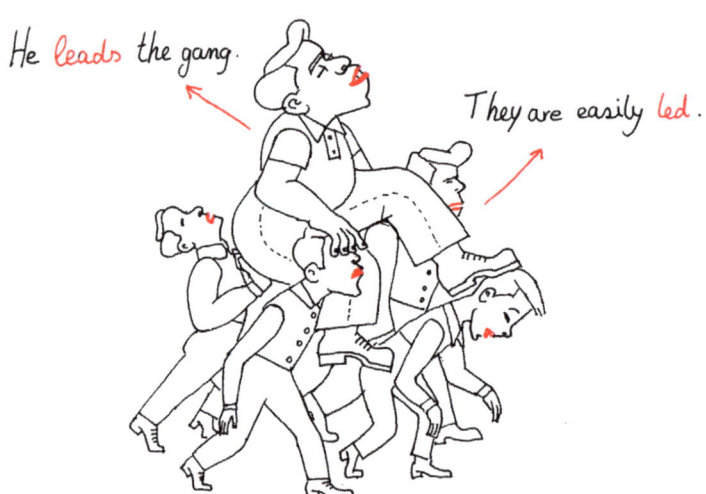

He *leads* the gang.

They are easily *led*.

TO LEAD | LEAD LED LED

TO LEND – LEND – LENT – LENT & BORROW
ribbon
necklace

Mrs. Sharp <u>borrowed</u> a little thing from Mr. Sharp. Mr. Sharp didn't want to <u>lend</u> it to her. She pretended to understand, but she didn't. When night came and the snores of Mr. Sharp got louder, she raised the knife... and cut! Then she could sleep soundly.

infinitive	past simple	past participle	meaning
LEAD	LED	LED	show the way by going ahead
LEAP	LEAPED | LEAPT	LEAPED | LEAPT	jump
LEAVE	LEFT	LEFT	go out of or far away from
LEND	LENT	LENT	allow the use of sth. temporarily
LET	LET	LET	allow
LIE	LAY	LAIN	assume a horizontal position
LIGHT	LIT | LIGHTED	LIT | LIGHTED	illuminate
LOSE	LOST	LOST	cease to have or retain sth.
MAKE	MADE	MADE	create | construct
MEAN	MEANT	MEANT	intend to convey | signify
MEET	MET	MET	come into the presence of someone
PAY	PAID	PAID	give money due for goods or services
PROVE	PROVED	PROVED | PROVEN	demonstrate the truth
PUT	PUT	PUT	place in a specified location
QUIT	QUIT	QUIT	stop an activity | leave a job
READ	READ	READ	grasp the meaning of written characters
RIDE	RODE	RIDDEN	travel and control a vehicle or horse
RING	RANG	RUNG	surround | make a bell sound
RISE	ROSE	RISEN	go up | increase
RUN	RAN	RUN	move fast on foot
SAY	SAID	SAID	express in words
SEE	SAW	SEEN	perceive with the eyes
SEEK	SOUGHT	SOUGHT	try to locate | search for
SELL	SOLD	SOLD	give in exchange for money
SEND	SENT	SENT	cause to be taken to a destination

infinitive	past simple	past participle	meaning
SET	SET	SET	put in a specified position or state
SEW	SEWED	SEWED | SEWN	stitch with needle and thread
SHAKE	SHOOK	SHAKEN	move with jerky movements
SHAVE	SHAVED	SHAVED | SHAVEN	cut hair off with a razor
SHINE	SHONE | SHINED	SHONE | SHINED	emit light
SHOOT	SHOT	SHOT	fire a bullet from a weapon
SHOW	SHOWED	SHOWN	cause or allow to be seen
SHRINK	SHRANK | SHRUNK	SHRUNK | SHRUNKEN	become smaller
SHUT	SHUT	SHUT	move sth. to block passage
SING	SANG	SUNG	make musical sounds with the voice
SINK	SANK | SUNK	SUNK	submerge
SIT	SAT	SAT	rest one's weight on the buttocks
SLEEP	SLEPT	SLEPT	rest one's body and mind
SLIDE	SLID	SLID	move smoothly over a surface
SPEAK	SPOKE	SPOKEN	talk
SPEED	SPED | SPEEDED	SPED | SPEEDED	move quickly
SPEND	SPENT	SPENT	pay out money
SPILL	SPILLED | SPILT	SPILLED | SPILT	allow a liquid to fall out of its container
SPIN	SPUN	SPUN	rotate quickly
SPIT	SPIT | SPAT	SPAT	eject from the mouth
SPLIT	SPLIT	SPLIT	divide into parts
SPREAD	SPREAD	SPREAD	open wider | extend
SPRING	SPRANG	SPRUNG	move upward or forward
STAND	STOOD	STOOD	maintain an upright position
STEAL	STOLE	STOLEN	take without permission or right

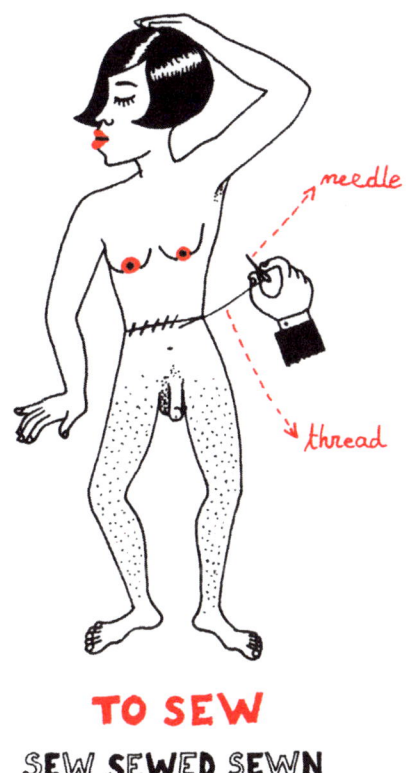

needle

thread

TO SEW
SEW SEWED SEWN

Mr. Smith <u>sewed</u> half of his pretty neighbor's body and half of his nice butcher's body together. Now he has the perfect wife. Or does he have the perfect husband?

TO STICK
STICK·STUCK·STUCK

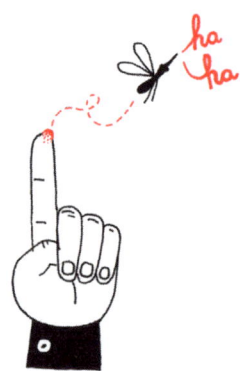

TO STING
STING-STUNG-STUNG

TO SWEEP
SWEEP-SWEPT-SWEPT

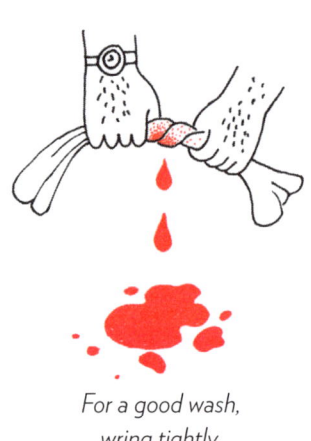

*For a good wash,
wring tightly.*

TO WRING
WRING-WRUNG-WRUNG

infinitive	past simple	past participle	meaning
STICK	STUCK	STUCK	pierce, puncture
STING	STUNG	STUNG	prick painfully
STINK	STANK	STUNK	emit bad smell
STRIKE	STRUCK	STRUCK	hit with the hand or a weapon
SWEAR	SWORE	SWORN	make a solemn statement or promise
SWEEP	SWEPT	SWEPT	clean with a broom
SWIM	SWAM	SWUM	move through water
SWING	SWUNG	SWUNG	move back and forth suspended
TAKE	TOOK	TAKEN	grasp with the hands | consume
TEACH	TAUGHT	TAUGHT	show or explain how to do sth.
TEAR	TORE	TORN	pull apart by force
TELL	TOLD	TOLD	communicate by speech or writing
THINK	THOUGHT	THOUGHT	formulate in the mind
THROW	THREW	THROWN	propel through the air
TREAD	TRODE	TRODDEN	step on
UNDERSTAND	UNDERSTOOD	UNDERSTOOD	comprehend meaning
UPSET	UPSET	UPSET	make someone distressed
WAKE UP	WOKE UP	WOKEN UP	emerge from a state of sleep
WEAR	WORE	WORN	carry or have on one's body
WEAVE	WOVE | WEAVED	WOVEN | WEAVED	make by interlacing threads
WEEP	WEPT	WEPT	cry
WIN	WON	WON	be successful or victorious
WITHDRAW	WITHDREW	WITHDRAWN	take back or away
WRING	WRUNG	WRUNG	twist to extract liquid
WRITE	WROTE	WRITTEN	form letters on a surface

lesson

PRESENT CONTINUOUS

SUBJECT + SIMPLE PRESENT "TO BE" + PRESENT PARTICIPLE (verb+ing)

I'm freezing...

WE ARE CELEBRATING THE CHINESE NEW YEAR. THIS IS THE YEAR OF THE SNAKE.

PRESENT CONTINUOUS
NEGATIVE

SUBJECT + SIMPLE PRESENT "TO BE" + NOT + PRESENT PARTICIPLE (verb+ing)

I'm not freezing...

PRESENT CONTINUOUS
QUESTION

SIMPLE PRESENT "TO BE" + SUBJECT + PRESENT PARTICIPLE (verb+ing)

Are you freezing?

SiMPLE PRESENT vs. PRESENT CONTiNUOUS

USE THE SIMPLE PRESENT for actions that happen regularly or things that do not often change, like opinions.
USE THE PRESENT CONTINUOUS for temporary actions happening now or definite plans for the future.

PAST CONTINUOUS

SUBJECT + SIMPLE PAST "TO BE" + PRESENT PARTICIPLE (VERB+ING)

I was telling...

PAST CONTINUOUS
NEGATIVE

SUBJECT + SIMPLE PAST "TO BE" + NOT + PRESENT PARTICIPLE (VERB+ING)

I was not telling...

PAST CONTINUOUS
QUESTION

SIMPLE PAST "TO BE" + SUBJECT + PRESENT PARTICIPLE (VERB+ING)

Was I telling....?

I like apples. Sometimes they come with a prize. Yesterday when I was eating one, a long squirmy thing appeared from inside after I took a bite. It was yummy.

A prize! Just like this one.

SIMPLE PAST vs. PAST CONTINUOUS

USE THE SIMPLE PAST for finished actions in the past.
USE THE PRESENT CONTINUOUS for actions in progress at a specific moment in the past.

The Tale
of the young foreign girl

Once upon a time, a young foreign girl *was looking* for a room in New York City. Nobody *wanted* her in their apartment. Her problem *was* that she *didn't speak* English!

When the young foreign girl *was* desperate, after days and weeks of visiting rooms all over the city and talking with potential roommates, she *found* her chance. One rainy morning she *met* with a man who *was looking* for a roommate. It *seemed* he *didn't care* about her poor English.

They *met* in the busiest downtown coffee shop. He *was* quite a lot older than her. He *was wearing* all black with black-rimmed glasses over a big nose. He *looked* like an ordinary guy. They both *ordered* a cup of tea and sat at a small table.

He *was* very interested in the young girl's life. He *didn't stop* asking questions. She *tried* to explain, with her limited knowledge of the language and some gestures, why she *was* in the city and what she *did* for a living.

Satisfied with her answers, he *started* to talk about the apartment. It *sounded* great! Nice place, nice price and friendly roommate. She <u>was</u> grateful for her good luck. Her troubles <u>were</u> over, she <u>thought</u>.

Then the guy <u>showed</u> her some crumpled pictures of a big bright room, a spacious, charming living room, and a clean, tidy kitchen. Meanwhile, he <u>was getting</u> closer to her and he said:

"But there are some conditions. First, you can't have friends over for the first two weeks. Second, you have to be nice to me."

"Well, I'm nice," the young foreigner <u>said</u>. "Why the first condition?"

"Because we will get to know each other faster and it will be easier for us to become friends, close friends," the guy <u>said</u>, smiling. "And there is one more condition. If you are a bad girl, I will beat your young little ass."

So the young foreign girl <u>ran</u> away. Even with her limited English, she <u>understood</u>. She is still looking for a room in New York City, visiting apartments and talking with potential roommates... for who knows how long..

lesson

ADJECTIVES

TALL   SHORT

FAT   SLIM

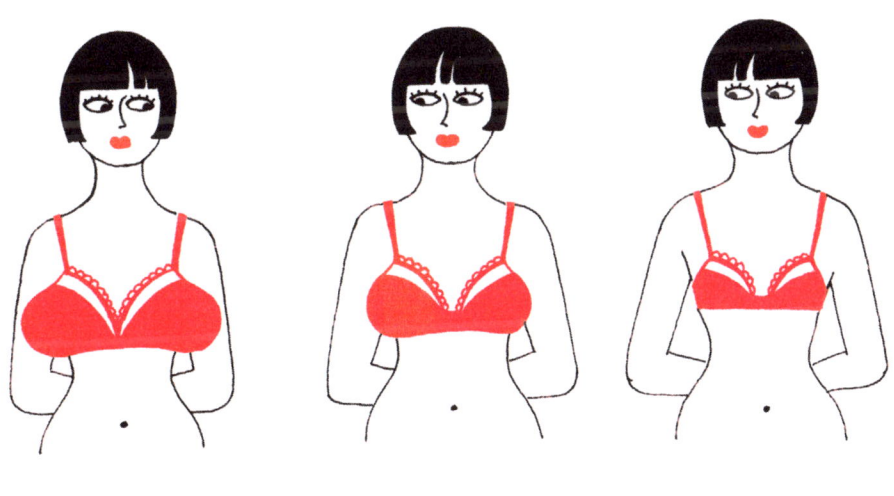

BIG   MEDIUM   SMALL

ADJECTIVES
provide information about nouns.

They come before the noun:
Thank God, the <u>chatty parrot</u> is sleeping. (~~the parrot chatty~~)

They don't change depending on number:
Blacky is my <u>black cat</u>.
I have eight <u>black cats</u> and I'm still lucky.

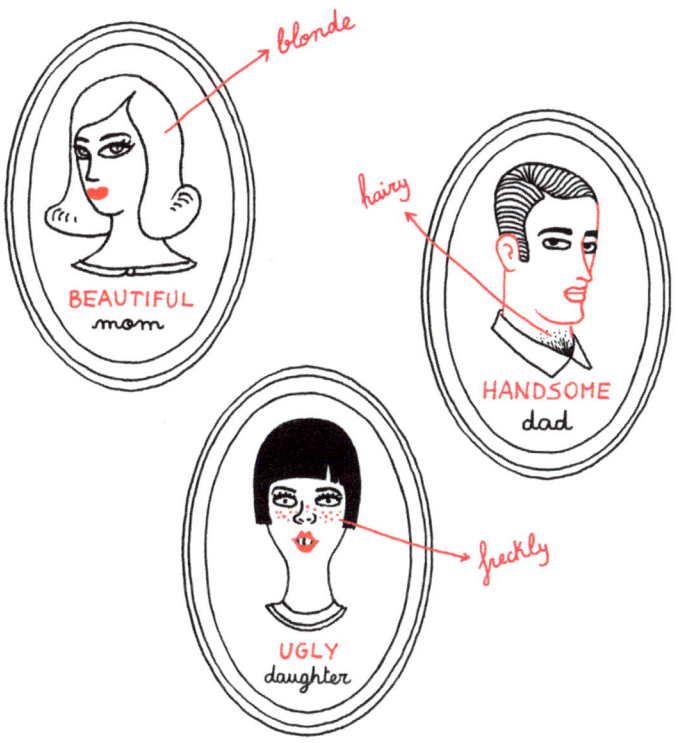

blonde

BEAUTIFUL
mom

hairy

HANDSOME
dad

freckly

UGLY
daughter

Life is full of surprises!

POLITE

DISHONEST

I'm honest

YOU CAN BE...

ARROGANT: having an exaggerated sense of one's own importance or abilities.
BRAVE: possessing courage.
CALM: not feeling nervous.
CLEVER: showing sharp intelligence.
CRAZY: affected with madness.

GRUMPY

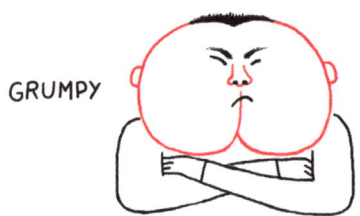

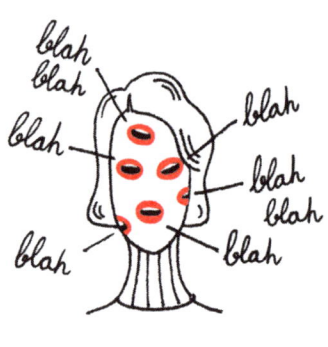

blah blah blah blah blah blah blah blah blah

CHATTY

WISE

DISTRUSTFUL

WEIRD

ENTHUSIASTIC: having great excitement and interest.
ENVIOUS: painfully desiring what someone else has.
FRIENDLY: warm, comforting.
FUNNY: causing laughter or amusement.

LONELY: without companions, solitary.
NICE: kind, friendly.
SARCASTIC: using words in a sense that is contrary to their meaning.
SILLY: foolish, lacking common sense.
WITTY: using quick and inventive verbal humor.

OPTIMISTIC

TOUGH

CHEEKY

JEALOUS

GOSSIPY

GIRLY

LAZY

NUTS

BUT WICKED

SHY

VAIN

SELFISH

SILLY

GLUTTONOUS

PERVERTED

UPSET - ANGRY

SAD

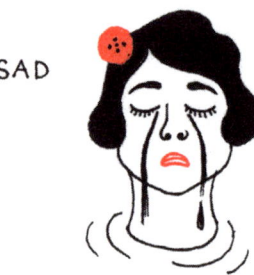

YOU CAN FEEL...

ANXIOUS: experiencing worry,
unease or nervousness.
ASHAMED: feeling
embarrasment.
COOL: having a moderately
low temperature.

WARM

HOT

 HAPPY

 TENSE

 DEPRESSED

DISTURBED: showing signs or symptoms of mental or emotional illness.
DIZZY: having a sensation of losing one's balance.
HEALTHY: possessing good health.
ILL: unhealthy, sick.

SLEEPY: needing or feeling ready for sleep.
UNEASY: feeling troubled or uncomfortable.
WORRIED: feeling uneasy or concerned about something.

 COLD

 *mmm!* HUNGRY

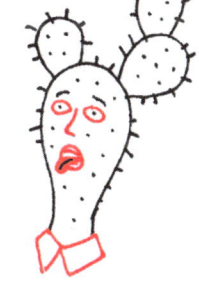 THIRSTY

PARTICIPIAL ADJECTIVES

are adjectives that can end in ED and ING.

Adjectives **ENDING IN ED**
describe how people feel.
Laura was <u>bored</u> by the movie.

Adjectives **ENDING IN ING**
describe how people or things are.
Laura didn't enjoy the movie because it was <u>boring</u>.

AMAZED AMAZING
feeling astonished causing astonishment

AMUSED AMUSING
feeling entertained causing entertainment

ANNOYED ANNOYING
feeling angry, irritated causing anger, irritation

BORED BORING
feeling tired and not interested not interesting, tedious

CONFUSED CONFUSING
feeling unable to understand causing disorientation

DISAPPOINTED DISAPPOINTING
feeling sad due to failed expectations not living up to expectations

EXCITED EXCITING
feeling enthusiastic causing enthusiasm

FRIGHTENED FRIGHTENING
feeling afraid causing fear

INTERESTED INTERESTING
feeling interest causing interest

IRRITATED IRRITATING
feeling irritation causing irritation

SURPRISED SURPRISING
feeling astonishment or shock causing astonishment or shock

THRILLED THRILLING
feeling intense pleasure and excitement causing intense pleasure and excitement

ADJECTIVE ORDER

When using more than one adjective,
you have to put them in the
RIGHT ORDER
according to type.

OPINION

SIZE

AGE

SHAPE

article | noun	1 OPINION	2 SIZE	3 AGE	4 SHAPE
a	silly	...	young	...
the	...	huge	...	round
my	lovely	...	...	...

 COLOR

 ORIGIN

 MATERIAL

 PURPOSE

5 COLOR	6 ORIGIN	7 MATERIAL	8 PURPOSE	noun
...	Spanish	...	...	man
...	...	wood	...	bowl
red	...	...	dancing	shoes

ADJECTIVE + PREPOSITION
EXPRESSIONS

Common **ADJECTIVES**
with the **PREPOSITIONS** that normally follow them:

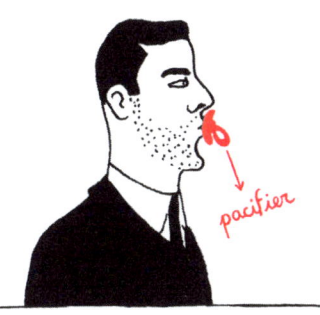

Everyone has a weakness, even those who look strong.
This guy is very **ATTACHED TO***his pacifier.

*fond of.

I'm
HOOKED ON*
coffee.

*addicted to.

I'm
FASCINATED BY*
science fiction.

*compelled by or attracted to.

ADDICTED TO
AFRAID OF
ANGRY AT
ANXIOUS ABOUT
ASHAMED OF
ATTACHED TO
AWARE OF
BAD AT
BORED WITH | BY
CAPABLE OF
CAREFUL OF
CONCERNED ABOUT
CRAZY ABOUT
CURIOUS ABOUT
DIFFERENT FROM
EXCITED ABOUT
FASCINATED BY
FED UP WITH
GLAD ABOUT
GOOD AT
HAPPY ABOUT
HOOKED ON
INTERESTED IN
NERVOUS ABOUT
OBSESSED WITH
PROUD OF
READY FOR
SAFE FROM
SATISFIED WITH
SICK OF
SORRY FOR | ABOUT
TERRIBLE AT
TIRED OF
WORRIED ABOUT

COMPARATIVES

ONE SYLLABLE: .... *old* .... add ER .... *older* ....

ending in consonant

after a vowel: .... *big* .... double the consonant and add ER ..... *bigger* ....

TWO SYLLABLES: .... *careful* .... use MORE before the adjective .... *more careful* ....

ending in Y: .... *happy* .... change Y to I and add ER .... *happier* ....

ending in ER, LE, OW: ... *narrow* .... add ER .... *narrower* ....

THREE OR MORE

SYLLABLES: .... *beautiful* ..... use MORE before the adjective .... *more beautiful* ....

SUPERLATIVES

I AM THE BEST

YOU ARE
THE MOST
HANDSOME

YOU ARE
THE NICEST

THE CUTEST
GUY !

add EST	*oldest*
double the consonant and add EST	*biggest*
use MOST before the adjective	*most careful*
change Y to I and add EST	*happiest*
add EST	*narrowest*
use MOST before the adjective	*most beautiful*

EXCEPTIONS:

good-better-best
bad-worse-worst
far-farther-farthest
little-less-least
many-more-most

AS ... AS

"As" is used to compare things that are
EQUAL:
She is <u>as old as</u> me | I (am).

It can also be used in negatives and questions:
I'm not <u>as stupid as</u> her | she (is).
Is she <u>as beautiful as</u> me | I (am)?

lesson

Adverbs

An **ADVERB**
modifies a verb, an adjective or another adverb.

It indicates how, where, when, why or under what conditions
something happens.

She <u>always</u> goes to the café in the <u>afternoon</u> <u>where</u> she has a cup of tea,
<u>probably</u> <u>after</u> spending <u>too</u> <u>much</u> time outside.
<u>Surely</u> she is sad.
Or <u>maybe</u> <u>simply</u> tired.

PUFF!

time adverbs

HOW OFTEN: *sometimes, frequently, never, often, yearly*
FOR HOW LONG: *all day, not long, for a while, since last year*
WHEN: *today, yesterday, later, now, last year*

SHE IS PREGNANT NOW.

WHEN adverbs are usually placed at the end of the sentence.

SHE HAS BEEN PREGNANT FOR NINE MONTHS.

FOR HOW LONG adverbs are usually placed at the end of the sentence.

SHE HAS OFTEN HAD STRANGE CRAVINGS DURING HER PREGNANCIES.

HOW OFTEN adverbs are usually placed before the main verb but after auxiliary verbs. **HOW OFTEN** adverbs that express the exact number of times an action happens are usually placed at the end of the sentence.

SHE HAS BEEN PREGNANT FOR NINE MONTHS EVERY YEAR FOR THE LAST DECADE.

Order for more than one adverb describing time: FOR HOW LONG, HOW OFTEN, WHEN

interrogative adverbs

why, where, how, when

relative adverbs

where, when, why

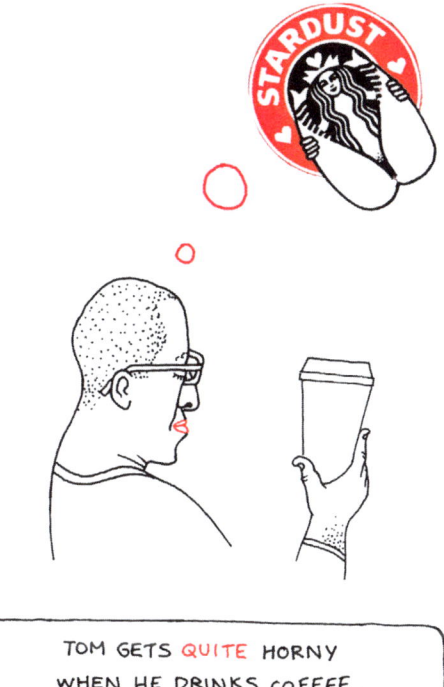

TOM GETS QUITE HORNY
WHEN HE DRINKS COFFEE.

Adverbs of degree are usually placed
before the main verb, or before the
adjective or adverb they modify.

aduerbs of degree

almost, nearly, just, too, enough, hardly, completely, very

Place adverbs usually go after the main verb.

...or after the object.

place adverbs

everywhere, away, up, down, around, out, back, in, outside

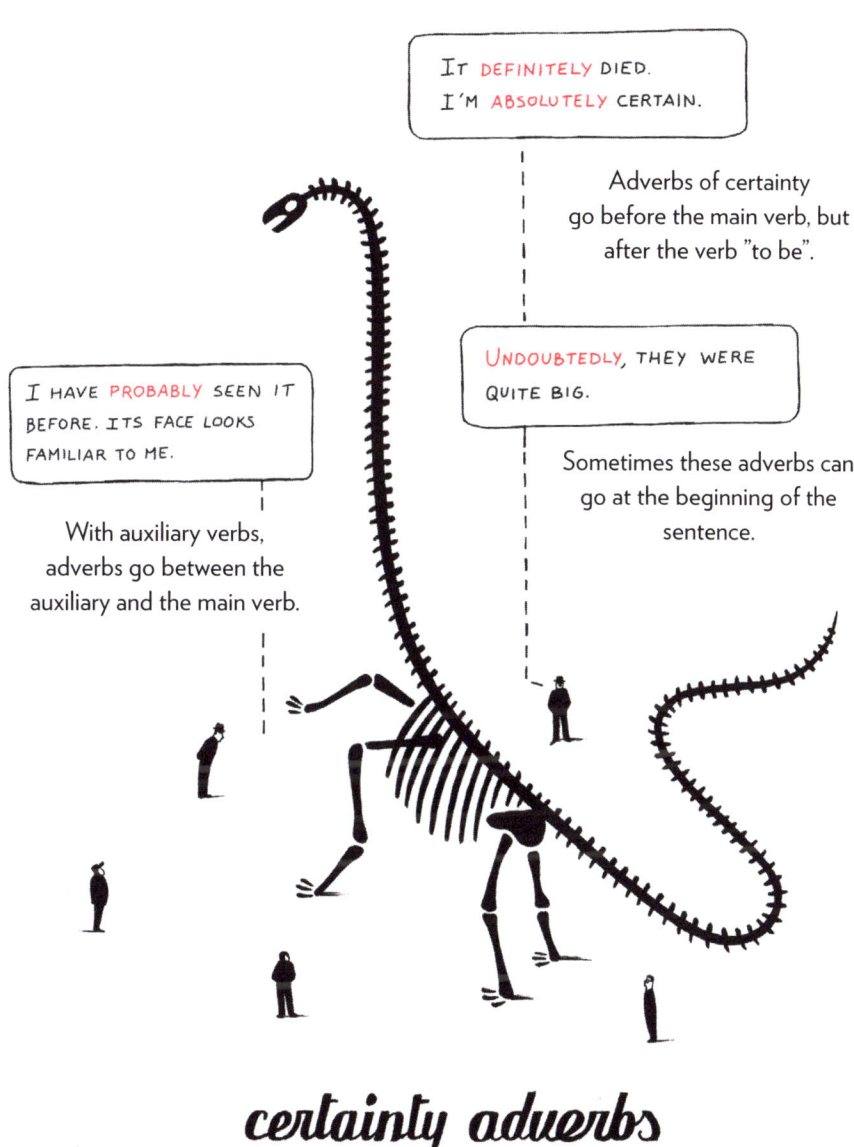

It DEFINITELY DIED.
I'M ABSOLUTELY CERTAIN.

Adverbs of certainty
go before the main verb, but
after the verb "to be".

UNDOUBTEDLY, THEY WERE
QUITE BIG.

Sometimes these adverbs can
go at the beginning of the
sentence.

I HAVE PROBABLY SEEN IT
BEFORE. ITS FACE LOOKS
FAMILIAR TO ME.

With auxiliary verbs,
adverbs go between the
auxiliary and the main verb.

certainty adverbs

certainly, definitely, probably, undoubtedly, surely

manner adverbs

well, rapidly, slowly, quickly, easily, loudly, softly, beautifully

SHE SPENDS HER SALARY QUICKLY.
SHE SPENDS IT EASILY.

Manner adverbs usually go after the main verb or the object.

SHE HAPPILY BETS AGAINST THE MACHINE.

To emphasize, manner adverbs can go before the verb if it's a transitive verb.

Commenting adverbs are very similar to viewpoint adverbs, but they go after the verb "to be" and before the main verb.

Viewpoint adverbs go at the beginning of the sentence, and are separated from the rest of the sentence by a comma.

I THINK SHE IS CERTAINLY THE WORST PERSON I HAVE EVER KNOWN. DON'T YOU THINK?

FRANKLY, MY DEAR, I DON'T GIVE A DAMN.

viewpoint adverbs

honestly, frankly, personally, obviously, surely, undoubtedly

and commenting adverbs

definitely, certainly, obviously, simply

IN, ON, AT
place prepositions

IN	**ON**	**AT**
inside an area or space	in contact with a surface	referring to a position
in the city	on the table	at the corner
in New York	on the wall	at the end of the street
in bed	on the floor	at the entrance
in my pocket	on the carpet	at the station
in the car	on the door	at the top of the page

TALKING ABOUT TRANSPORTATION:
in a | the: *car, truck*
on a | the: *subway, bus, train, airplane, ship, bicycle*

COMMON EXPRESSIONS:
in: *in a car, in a taxi, in an elevator, in the newspaper, in the sky, in Times Square*
on: *on a bus, on a train, on an airplane, on the radio, on the Internet, on the left*
at: *at home, at work, at school, at college, at the bottom, at the reception*

iN, ON, AT

time prepositions

IN	ON	AT
months, seasons, years, centuries	days and dates	hours of the clock, points in time
in April	*on Sunday*	*at 5 o'clock*
in summer	*on Mondays*	*at noon | night*
in 1900 | in the 1900s	*on September the 4th*	*at bedtime*
in the past century	*on his birthday*	*at the moment*
in the future	*on New Year's Eve*	*at the end of the week*

COMMON EXPRESSIONS:

in: *in the morning(s), in the afternoon(s), in the evening(s)*
on: *on Tuesday morning(s), on Wednesday afternoon(s), on weekends*
at: *at night, at Christmas, at the same time*

When using LAST, NEXT, EVERY or THIS,
don't use "in", "on" or "at":
I was depressed last May (not ~~in last May~~)
I'm planning to rob a bank next Monday (not ~~on next Monday~~)
I eat donuts every Christmas (not ~~at every Christmas~~)
I will take a walk naked this evening (not ~~in this evening~~)

lesson 9

TiCK ToCK

• WHAT TIME IS IT? •

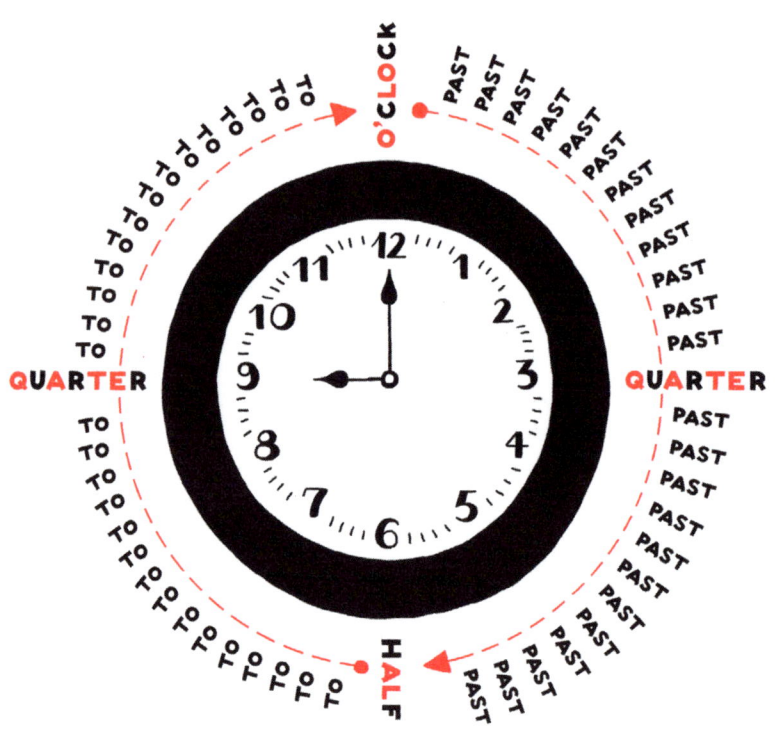

A QUARTER PAST SEVEN

TWENTY PAST EIGHT

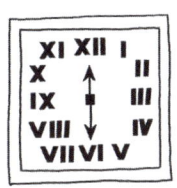

HALF PAST TWELVE
OR
TWELVE THIRTY

A QUARTER TO TWO

SIX O'CLOCK

FIVE TO FOUR

Helena is waiting for her lover.
They had a date at <u>a quarter to eight</u>.
She is still waiting for him.

Claudine arranged a date with the guy
who has been giving her flowers for the last
two months. The date was at <u>seven o'clock</u>.
She won't be getting any more flowers.

The guy who Jennifer is waiting for should
have arrived at a _quarter past eight_. He is
fifteen minutes late so far. Perhaps she will
be luckier than the other two girls.

Waiting in a café

★ during the day ★

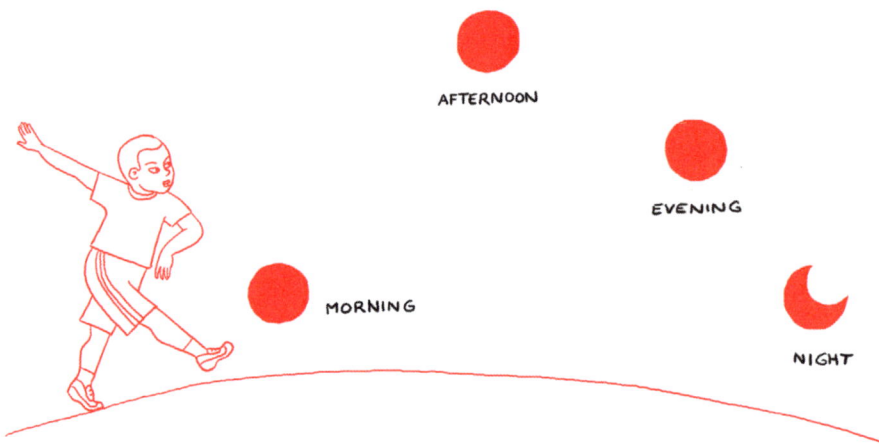

AFTERNOON

EVENING

MORNING

NIGHT

GREETINGS:
GOOD MORNING: from the time you wake up until 12 p.m.
GOOD AFTERNOON: from 12 p.m. (or after lunch) to 5 p.m.
GOOD EVENING: after 5 p.m.
GOOD NIGHT: to say goodbye at night or before going to bed.

———————————————

12 p.m. = noon or midday | 12 a.m.= midnight
After 11 a.m. follows 12 p.m., so after 11 p.m. follows 12 a.m.
A.M. means *ante meridiem* (before noon). P.M. means *post meridiem* (after noon).

DAYS OF THE WEEK:

The days of the week start with a capital letter.

Sunday
Monday
Tuesday
Wednesday
Thursday
Friday
Saturday

SABBATH !

—MONTHS—

THE 4 SEASONS

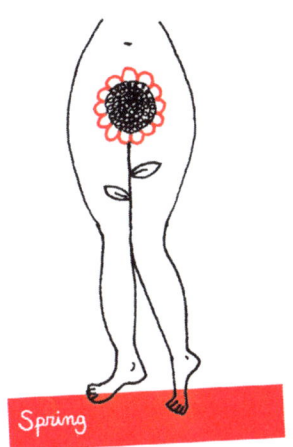

Spring

Summer

Fall

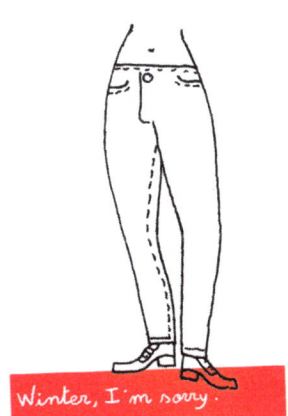

Winter, I'm sorry.

WHAT'S THE DATE?

dates in written English

September 4, 2007

4th September, 2007 → Br. English

September 4th, 2007 → Am. English

9/4/07

dates in spoken English

September fourth, two thousand and seven.

September the fourth, two thousand and seven.

The fourth of September, two thousand and seven.

lesson

10

THE FUTURE
is WILL

SUBJECT + WILL + INFINITIVE without "to"
I will love...

The future **WILL**
is used for future predictions and facts.

I will have seven children. I will get married to a rich and handsome man. My wonderful husband will love me very much. He will sow seven seeds in me, from which seven children will grow. Seven is my lucky number. Blue is my favorite color. But what I like most is pizza.

WILL
is also used :

To make a SPONTANEOUS RESPONSE.
The telephone is ringing. I will answer it!

To mean WANT TO or BE WILLING TO.
I hope you will come to my apartment tonight.

In reference to OFFERS and PROMISES.
I will bring some food.
She always says she will cook, but she is a disaster when it comes to cooking.

FUTURE WILL
question

WILL + SUBJECT + INFINITIVE without "to"
Will you be....?

SUBJECT + WILL NOT | WON'T + INFINITIVE without "to"

I won't grow up!

FUTURE WILL
negative

the other future:
be going to

SUBJECT + TO BE + GOING TO + VERB
I'm going to dance...

The future
BE GOING TO
is used to describe
FUTURE PLANS
and **INTENTIONS.**

I'M GOING TO LEAVE MY JOB.

I'M GOING TO GIVE AWAY MY STUFF.

I'M GOING TO DANCE EVERY NIGHT.

I'M GOING TO GO TO THE CONGO.

The future **BE GOING TO**
is also used to make a
PREDICTION
based on present evidence.
*She is going to stay the same and
forget about all her plans.*

GOING TO = GONNA
in spoken English

SUBJECT + TO BE + NOT + GOING + INFINITIVE
She's not going to accomplish her plans.

TO BE + SUBJECT + GOING + INFINITIVE
Is she going to stop complaining?

★ **FUTURE** CONTINUOUS ★

SUBJECT + WILL BE + PRESENT PARTICIPLE (verb+ing)

I will be waiting...

Use Future Continuous:

When an **ACTION** will be
IN PROGRESS IN THE FUTURE.

She'll be waiting until her husband arrives.

I'LL BE WAITING UP FOR YOU AWAKE.

I'LL BE ARRIVING AROUND 10 P.M.

For an **ACTION IN THE FUTURE**
that happens
AROUND A CERTAIN TIME.

Next year they will be enjoying their mornings just as much.

For **FORMAL OFFERS**.

Will you be eating some appetizers, madam?
Yes, I will. Mmm... delicious!

To **CHECK INFORMATION**.

Will you be having lunch with us?
Sure! Will you be going to the party later?

For **SYMPATHETIC PREDICTIONS**
about people's feelings.
You'll be needing to unwind after a hard day of work.
I'm going to be needing a blossom tea.

★ **FUTURE** CONTINUOUS ★
negatives

SUBJECT + WILL NOT BE | WON'T BE + PRESENT PARTICIPLE (verb+ing)
She won't be waiting...

or with **BE GOING TO**

SUBJECT + IS | ARE+ NOT + GOING TO BE + PRESENT PARTICIPLE (verb+ing)
She's not going to be waiting...

★ FUTURE CONTINUOUS ★
questions

WILL BE + SUBJECT + PRESENT PARTICIPLE (verb+ing)
Will you be needing...?

or with **BE GOING TO**

TO BE + SUBJECT + GOING TO BE + PRESENT PARTICIPLE (verb+ing)
Are you going to be needing...?

lesson 11

simple PRESENT PERFECT

SUBJECT + HAVE | HAS + PAST PARTICIPLE

I have spent...

I have been happily married <u>since</u> I met this man.

I have spent my parents' savings.

With **HOW LONG | FOR | SINCE** for verbs not normally used in continuous forms: BE, HAVE, KNOW, LIKE.

For **COMPLETED ACTIONS** when no time is given.

I have not <u>ever</u> been to Miami.

I have had <u>six</u> <u>beers</u>.

It's the <u>best</u> feeling I've <u>ever</u> had in my whole life.

With **EVER | ALREADY YET | JUST**.

When we say **HOW MANY** or **HOW MANY TIMES**.

With **SUPERLATIVES**.

PRESENT PERFECT *continuous*

SUBJECT + HAVE | HAS + BEEN + PRESENT PARTICIPLE (verb+ing)

I have been cheating...

For continuous actions, epecially for questions with **HOW LONG** and answers with **FOR | SINCE**.

For **CONTINUOUS ACTIONS** recently finished.

simple PRESENT PERFECT

negative

SUBJECT + HAVEN'T | HASN'T + PAST PARTICIPLE

I haven't forgotten...

question

HAVE | HAS + SUBJECT + PAST PARTICIPLE

Have you lost...?

PRESENT PERFECT *continuous*

negative

SUBJECT + HAVEN'T | HASN'T + BEEN + PRESENT PARTICIPLE (verb+ing)

I haven't been eating...

question

HAVE | HAS + SUBJECT + BEEN + PRESENT PARTICIPLE (verb+ing)

Have you been eating?

PRESENT PERFECT *or* SIMPLE PAST?

The **SIMPLE PAST**

is usually used for finished actions with a past time expression
(yesterday, ago, last week...).

I always <u>thought</u> dinosaurs were just science fiction.
= she doesn't think so anymore.

The **PRESENT PERFECT**

is usually used if an action started in the past and is still going on now.

<u>*I have believed*</u> *in the existence of dinosaurs since I met you.*
= he still believes they exist.

simple PAST PERFECT

SUBJECT + HAD + PAST PARTICIPLE

I had fallen...

To talk about
an **ACTION** that happened
BEFORE ANOTHER EVENT
in the past.

Adverbs describing time
(already, just, never, ever, before)
are commonly used.

*She had never fallen off her bike before the
time when she broke her leg.*

Also used in
REPORTED SPEECH.
She whispered what they had said.

Past Perfect continuous

SUBJECT + HAD BEEN + PRESENT PARTICIPLE (verb+ing)

She had been dancing...

To talk about
AN ACTION that started in the past
and **CONTINUED UP
UNTIL ANOTHER EVENT**
in the past.

*She <u>had been dancing</u> until her back said
"stop".*

simple PAST PERFECT

negative

SUBJECT + HADN'T + PAST PARTICIPLE

I hadn't felt...

question

HAD + SUBJECT + PAST PARTICIPLE

Had you been...?

Past Perfect *continuous*

negative

SUBJECT + HADN'T + BEEN + PRESENT PARTICIPLE (verb+ing)

I hadn't been stealing...

question

HAD + SUBJECT + BEEN + PRESENT PARTICIPLE (verb+ing)

Had you been stealing?

simple FUTURE PERFECT

SUBJECT + WILL HAVE + PAST PARTICIPLE

I will have succeeded...

To show that
an **ACTION** will be **COMPLETED**
BY A CERTAIN TIME
in the future.
*He will have succeeded in making a friend
by the time he's no longer afraid of people.
When he makes a friend,
he will have overcome his fear of people.*

BY NEXT SPRING,
MAYBE I 'LL HAVE
SUCCEEDED IN
MAKING A FRIEND.

FUTURE PERFECT *continuous*

SUBJECT + WILL HAVE BEEN + PRESENT PARTICIPLE (verb+ing)

I will have been working...

To show how long
an **ACTIVITY** will be taking place
BEFORE ANOTHER
in the future.
*She will have been working for 16 hours
and she will still have to prepare dinner for
her husband.*

simple FUTURE PERFECT

negative

SUBJECT + WON'T HAVE + PAST PARTICIPLE

You won't have forgiven...

question

WILL + SUBJECT + HAVE + PAST PARTICIPLE

Will I have gotten...?

FUTURE PERFECT *continuous*

negative

SUBJECT + WON'T HAVE BEEN + PRESENT PARTICIPLE (verb+ing)

I won't have been wasting...

question

WILL + SUBJECT + HAVE BEEN + PRESENT PARTICIPLE (verb+ing)

Will I have been trying...?

PRESENT TENSES	PAST	PRESENT	FUTURE
SIMPLE PRESENT		*I want cookies.*	*The movie starts at 5 p.m.*
		I am silly.	
PRESENT CONTINUOUS		*I'm driving right now.*	*I'm meeting friends tonight.*
		I'm living in New York.	
SIMPLE PRESENT PERFECT	*I have been to Italy.*	*I have cleaned the room.*	
PRESENT PERFECT CONTINUOUS	*I have been drinking.*		
		I have been waiting in line for 2 hours.	

PAST TENSES	PAST	PRESENT	FUTURE
SIMPLE PAST	I _played_ with dolls.	If I _lied_ to you, you would know.	If you _forgot_ to bring it, I'd remind you.
PAST CONTINUOUS	I _was sleeping_ at 11 a.m.		If I _wasn't working_ tomorrow, I would go.
SIMPLE PAST PERFECT	I _had lost_ some weight.		
PAST PERFECT CONTINUOUS	I _had been crying_ all day.	If I _had been reading_, I wouldn't have seen you.	

FUTURE TENSES	PAST	PRESENT	FUTURE
SIMPLE FUTURE		I'_ll answer_ the phone.	I _will buy_ the tickets tomorrow.
FUTURE CONTINUOUS			I _will be having_ dinner with friends.
FUTURE SIMPLE PERFECT			I _will have finished_.
	I _will have lived_ here for five years next week.		
FUTURE PERFECT CONTINUOUS			I'_ll have been waiting_ for 2 hours when you arrive.
	Soon, I _will have been driving_ for 12 hours.		

lesson

12

GERUND	TO + INFINITIVE
After **PREPOSITIONS**.	After **ADJECTIVES**.
I'm tired of <u>running.</u>	*This problem is difficult <u>to solve</u>.*
After **CERTAIN VERBS**:	After **CERTAIN VERBS**:
like, love, hate, enjoy, mind, finish, stop.	would like, want, need, decide, hope,
I enjoy <u>seeing</u> you.	expect, plan, forget, seem, try, promise,
	offer, refuse, learn, manage.
As the **SUBJECT** of a sentence	*I would like <u>to escape</u>.*
<u>Smoking</u> *is a pleasure.*	
	To express **PURPOSE | REASON**.
	I'm chasing this guy <u>to earn</u> my bread and
	butter.

• USUALLY •
• USED TO •
• BE USED TO •
• GET USED TO •

USUALLY

FOR CURRENT HABITS

subject + USUALLY + verb

Melissa, a good English teacher, usually makes students repeat sentences correctly. This <u>usually</u> bothers Meritxell, her student, a little.

USED TO

FOR PAST HABITS OR PAST SITUATIONS THAT HAVE CHANGED

subject + USED TO + infinitive

Meritxell <u>used to</u> take drugs, but now she doesn't even smoke.

BE USED TO

FOR A NEW SITUATION THAT YOU ARE ALREADY ACCUSTOMED TO

subject + BE USED TO + gerund or noun

Melissa <u>is used to</u> craving food all the time since she quit smoking.

GET USED TO

FOR SOMETHING THAT IS BECOMING FAMILIAR TO YOU
OR TO WHICH YOU ARE ADAPTING.

subject + GET USED TO + gerund or noun

Melissa and Meritxell <u>haven't gotten used to</u> living without addictions.

WISH is commonly used to express regret or in reference to unreal situations.
Wishes for the **PRESENT** and **FUTURE**:

Use **PAST SIMPLE**
to express when you would like a
situation to be different.
He wishes she were here.

Use **PAST CONTINUOUS**
to express when you would like to be
doing something different.
He wishes they were lying on the bed.

You can use "were" for I | he | she | it.

Wishes for the
PAST:

Use **PAST PERFECT**
to express regret or when you would like
a situation to be different.
He wishes she hadn't come over.

To **COMPLAIN**
or express **IMPATIENCE**:

Use **WOULD + VERB**
He wishes she would stop laughing.
or **COULD + VERB**
He wishes he could make her disappear.

You can use **SUBJECT + WISH + PRONOUN** in fixed expressions: *I wish you the best.*

RATHER

is used to express **PREFERENCE**.

RATHER THAN

means "instead of" or "and not".
Normally used to compare
parallel structures.

> HE IS A SEX MANIAC RATHER THAN
> AN ART ENTHUSIAST.

WOULD RATHER... THAN

means "would prefer to..."
Used to show preference between options.
SUBJECT + WOULD RATHER + INFINITIVE without "to"
+ OPTION 1 + THAN + OPTION 2

> ELVIS WOULD RATHER
> BE THE CENTER OF ATTENTION
> THAN
> BE JUST LIKE EVERYBODY ELSE.

WOULD RATHER

means "would prefer".
Used to show preference for one option
over another.
SUBJECT + WOULD RATHER + INFINITIVE without "to"
+ OPTION

> – Hey Jeff! Let's get out of here!
> – I 'd rather stay here.

OR RATHER

Used to change what it is just said.

> She is distracted, or rather, she
> is pretending to be distracted.

RATHER

is also an adverb of degree.
It means "quite".

> Marilyn had a rather tender look.

CONNECTORS

Connectors, also called *linking words* or *linkers*,
indicate the relationship between ideas.

The last clue drove Harry to the wood house on top of the mountain. Maybe this would be the telltale clue. The weather was very bad and, in addition, the car lights didn't work because they had been shot out a couple of hours earlier. Despite all this, Harry managed to get to the place and get out of the car unnoticed. The lights of the house were on so Harry carefully crawled through the bushes until he reached the window. There he saw Elisabeth crying. Suddenly, a shiver came over his body. Instead of crying, Elisabeth was actually laughing and looking directly into Harry's eyes while holding the gun.

Types of connectors by meaning:

GIVING EXAMPLES
for example (e.g.), for instance, such as

INTRODUCING A TOPIC
with regard to, regarding, concerning, by the way

ADDING INFORMATION
and, also, too, as well as, in addition, apart from, besides, furthermore, moreover, then again

SUMMARIZING
in short, in brief, in summary, to conclude, in conclusion

GIVING A REASON
because, because of, for, since, as, due to, owing to

INTRODUCING DEVELOPMENTS
so, consequently, as a result, therefore, thus, hence

REFLECTING CONTRAST
but, however, although, even though, though, despite, in spite of, nevertheless, nonetheless, while, whereas, unlike, on the other hand, anyway

SEQUENCING IDEAS
firstly, secondly, thirdly, to begin with, next, lastly, finally

DURING THE NARRATIVE
at the beginning, then, at last, once, afterwards, suddenly, finally, in the end

EMPHASIZING
obviously, particularly, in theory, in fact, especially

SHOWING CERTAINTY
surely, indeed, undoubtedly, certainly, even so

A relative clause
is a dependent clause that modifies a word, phrase or idea in the main clause.

It begins with a **RELATIVE PRONOUN**:
WHO, WHOM, WHOSE, THAT or WHICH
(in certain situations, WHAT, WHEN and WHERE can function as relative pronouns)
The type of clause determines which relative pronoun to use.

There are two types of relative clauses:
NON-DEFINING CLAUSES and **DEFINING CLAUSES**.

NEWS

OCTOBER 1, 2007

35

The press, *which is threatened by rapidly changing technology*, is making a daily effort to keep its readers' interest or, rather, lack thereof.
Our newspaper has gotten in on the act too!

Defining Clauses

The information contained
in defining clauses is **ESSENTIAL**.
When deleted, it's not clear who or
what is being talked about.

In this type of clause
the relative pronouns used are:
For people: WHO, THAT
(and WHOM followed by a preposition)
For things: WHICH, THAT

This type of clause is
NOT separated by a **COMMA**.

*The woman <u>who is pushing a stroller</u>
is her heroine.*

Exercise, which is supposed to be good for your health, is killing me.

Non-Defining Clauses

In non-defining clauses
the information is **NOT ESSENTIAL**.
When deleted, it's still clear who or what
is being talked about.

In this type of clause
the relative pronouns used are:
For people: WHO
(and WHOM, WHOSE)
For things: WHICH (and WHOSE)

This type of clause is separated by
a **COMMA** from the main clause.

Exercise, <u>which is supposed to be good for your health</u>, is killing her.

ACTIVE & PASSIVE VOICES

There are two voices in English: the active and the passive.

The **ACTIVE VOICE**
describes what the subject does.
The dog bit Julianne's leg.

The **PASSIVE VOICE**
describes what is done to the subject.
It's usually used when we don't know
or are not interested in who performs the action.
Julianne's leg was bitten by some dog.

The passive voice is formed with:
TO BE + PAST PARTICIPLE
is made...

It can also be formed by:
TO GET + PAST PARTICIPLE
got broken...

All the verb tenses can be expressed in passive voice.
The concert <u>will be performed</u> next week.
The concert <u>has been performed</u> already.

BY is used
to show the person or thing doing the action.
The painting was made <u>by</u> a monkey.

THE PIGEONS ARE EATING A WORM.

WORMS ARE EATEN EVERY DAY
ALL OVER THE WORLD.

Reported Speech

There are two ways to repeat what another person said:
DIRECT SPEECH and **REPORTED SPEECH**.

DIRECT SPEECH
uses exact words in quotation marks.
She said "I need a friend".

_____

REPORTED SPEECH
is indirect.
She said she needed a friend.

Reported speech uses the past form of direct speech.
"I <u>need</u> a friend." - She said she <u>needed</u> a friend.
"I'<u>m feeling</u> alone." - She said she <u>was feeling</u> alone.
"I'<u>ve spent</u> all Sunday watching TV." - She said she <u>had spent</u> all Sunday watching TV.
"I <u>will go</u> to bed early." - She said she <u>would go</u> to bed early.

When direct speech uses a past form, reported speech doesn't change.
"I <u>was</u> afraid." - She said she <u>was</u> afraid.
"I <u>was looking</u> for a better life." - She said she <u>was looking</u> for a better life.

lesson 13

PHRASAL VERBS

Phrasal verbs are idiomatic expressions,
that combine
VERBS with **PREPOSITIONS** or **ADVERBS**
to make new verbs.

FACE UP TO

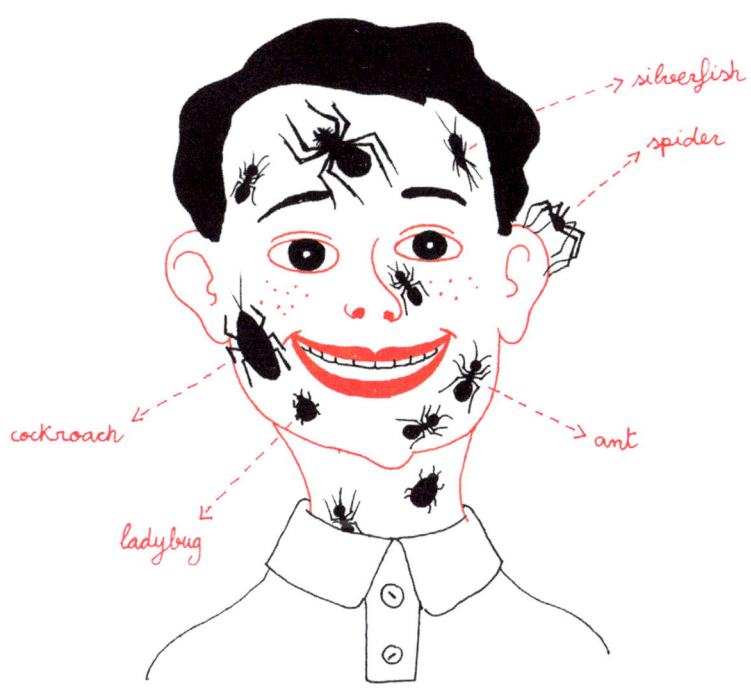

silverfish
spider
ant
cockroach
ladybug

= CONFRONT AND DEAL WITH

Billy Brave was afraid of bugs.
He decided to face up to his fear.

CREEP UP ON SOMEONE
also SNEAK UP ON SOMEBODY

= APPROACH GRADUALLY TO SURPRISE

You must creep up on your prey
if you don't want to be heard.

Some common phrasal verbs:

ACT UP	behave badly
ASK so. OVER	invite so. to your home
BLOW UP	explode
BLOW sth. UP	explode | fill with air | make sth. larger
BREAK DOWN	cease working | lose control
BRING sth. ABOUT	make happen
BRING sth. | so. BACK	revive
BRING so. DOWN	depress
BRING sth. UP	mention
CALL so. BACK	return a call
CALL sth. OFF	cancel
CALL so. UP	contact by phone
CARRY ON	continue
CATCH ON	understand, perceive | become popular
CHECK sth. OUT	examine
CHEER so. UP	make someone feel happier
CLEAN sth. | so. UP	clean a mess
CLEAR sth. UP	explain
CLOSE sth. DOWN	suspend or stop operations
COME BACK	return
COME IN	enter
COME OUT	be released publicly
COME UP WITH sth.	invent
COUNT ON sth. | so.	depend on
CREEP UP ON so.	approach gradually to surprise

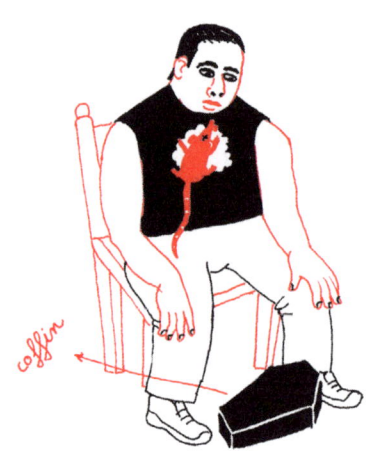

coffin

EAT AWAY AT

= GRADUALLY REDUCE OR DAMAGE

He killed a mouse and
that is *eating away at* his conscience.

CUT DOWN ON sth.	reduce
CUT sth. OUT	remove | stop
CUT sth. UP	cut into small pieces
DO sth. OVER	do again
DO sth. | so. UP	make more beautiful
DRAW sth. TOGETHER	unite
DREAM sth. UP	invent
DRESS UP	wear special clothes
DRINK sth. UP	drink completely
DROP IN	visit quickly, casually or without invitation
DROP sth. | so. OFF	deliver
EAT AWAY AT	gradually reduce or damage
EAT IN	eat at home
EAT OUT	eat at a restaurant | perform oral sex (on a woman)
END UP WITH sth.	get as a result
FACE UP TO	confront and deal with
FALL APART	break to pieces
FALL DOWN	fail to meet expectations
FALL FOR so.	fall in love with
FIGURE sth. | so. OUT	discover | solve | understand so.
FILL sth. IN	complete with information
FILL sth. OUT	complete a form with information
FIND sth. OUT	discover
FIX sth. UP	improve

FIND OUT

= DISCOVER

FALL APART

= BREAK TO PIECES

A woman with a vase fell down. The woman fell apart.
They used the vase as her funeral urn. It seemed safe.

FOLLOW THROUGH	complete
FOOL AROUND	act jokingly | engage in sexual foreplay
FREAK OUT	behave in a wild and irrational way
FUCK UP	make a mess, ruin or spoil
FUCK sth. **UP**	do sth. badly
FUCK so. **UP**	damage emotionally or physically
GIVE sth. **UP**	quit | abandon
GO ALONG WITH sth.	consent or agree to
GO BACK	return
GO DOWN	decrease
GO ON	continue
GO OUT	leave
GO UP	increase
GO OVER sth.	examine
GOBBLE DOWN	eat hungrily or quickly
GROW UP	become an adult
HANG OUT	spend time relaxing or socializing
HANG sth. **UP**	put on a hook or hanger
HANG UP	end a phone call
HOLD ON	wait | not hang up the phone
KEEP AWAY	stay at a distance
KEEP ON	continue
KEEP UP WITH	move at the same rate
LAY sth. **DOWN**	put sth. down horizontally
LAY sth. **OUT**	arrange according to a plan | spend money

FREAK OUT

= BEHAVE IN A WILD AND IRRATIONAL WAY

No matter how much she misses her husband,
every time she sees him she still freaks out.

LEAVE sth. **ON**	not to turn off or take off
LEAVE sth. | so. **OUT**	exclude
LET so. **DOWN**	disappoint
LET sth. | so. **IN**	allow to enter
LET so. **OFF**	not punish
LIE DOWN	recline
LIGHT UP	illuminate
LOOK AFTER	take care of
LOOK FOR	attempt to find
LOOK FORWARD TO	await eagerly
LOOK OUT	be careful
LOOK sth. **UP**	find information
MISS OUT	fail to use an opportunity
PASS sth. **UP**	refrain from accepting
PAY so. **BACK**	repay a loan
PAY OFF	be profitable
PICK sth. | so. **OUT**	choose from a group
PICK UP	improve | answer the phone
PICK sth. **UP**	collect sth. left elsewhere
PICK so. **UP**	go somewhere to collect so.
PISS so. **OFF**	annoy or make angry
PLAY AROUND	joke | have an affair
POINT sth. **OUT**	indicate
PUT sth. **AWAY**	save money | put sth. its proper place
PUT sth. **BACK**	return sth. to its original place

GOBBLE DOWN

= EAT HUNGRILY OR QUICKLY

Meryl was starving and didn't feel like cooking so she started *gobbling down* her beloved husband.

PISS SOMEONE OFF

= ANNOY OR MAKE ANGRY

Tamara is a calm girl,
but everything her mother says pisses her off.

PUT so. OFF	discourage | repulse
PUT sth. OFF	postpone
PUT sth. TOGETHER	assemble
PUT sth. UP	display for others to see
RIP so. OFF	cheat someone out of money
RUN INTO so.	meet by chance
SEND sth. BACK	return
SET sth. UP	place in position | prepare for use | arrange
SHUT UP	stop talking
SIGN so. UP	register
SIT DOWN	take a seat
SLIP UP	make a mistake
START sth. OVER	start again
STAY UP	remain awake
SWITCH sth. ON	start a machine or turn on a light
TAKE sth. AWAY	remove
TAKE sth. BACK	accept a return | retract words
TAKE sth. IN	comprehend fully
TAKE OFF	depart
TAKE sth. OFF	remove
TAKE so. ON	hire | challenge
TALK BACK	reply defiantly
TALK so. INTO	persuade
TALK sth. OVER	discuss
TEAR sth. DOWN | APART	destroy

TELL so. OFF	reprimand or scold | swear at so.
THINK BACK	remember the past
THINK sth. OVER	consider
THINK sth. UP	invent
THROW sth. AWAY	discard, put in the trash
THROW UP	vomit
TOUCH sth. UP	improve by making small changes
TRY sth. ON	put clothing on to see if it fits
TRY sth. OUT	use sth. to see if it works
TURN sth. DOWN	refuse | lower the volume
TURN so. DOWN	reject someone
TURN so. ON	excite someone sexually
TURN sth. | so. INTO	change from one form to another
TURN so. OFF	bore or offend so.
TURN sth. ON	start something (a machine, a light)
TURN so. ON	arouse someone sexually
TURN OUT	have a particular result
TURN UP	appear unexpectedly
TURN sth. UP	increase by adjusting the control on a device
WATCH OUT	be attentive
WAKE so. UP	stop sleeping
WORK sth. OFF	remove through work or other activity
WORK OUT	solve | exercise
WRITE sth. DOWN	write on a piece of paper

TRY SOMETHING ON
= PUT CLOTHING ON TO SEE IF IT FITS

He tried the gabardine on.
It was perfect for his exhibitionist habits.

PHRASAL VERBS with GET

Some phrasal verbs
can have numerous meanings,
especially phrasal verbs with the word GET!

GET ALONG

GET BACK AT SOMEONE

=TAKE REVENGE

I WILL GET BACK AT YOU!

GET BACK

= RETURN FROM
SOMEWHERE
= TAKE REVENGE
= MOVE AWAY

GET BACK INTO

= DEVOTE ONESELF TO
SOMETHING AGAIN

GET BACK TO

= RESPOND TO A
CONTACT
= START DOING sth. AFTER
AN INTERRUPTION

GET BACK TOGETHER
= RESTART A RELATIONSHIP

GET BACK INTO
= DEVOTE ONESELF TO SOMETHING AGAIN

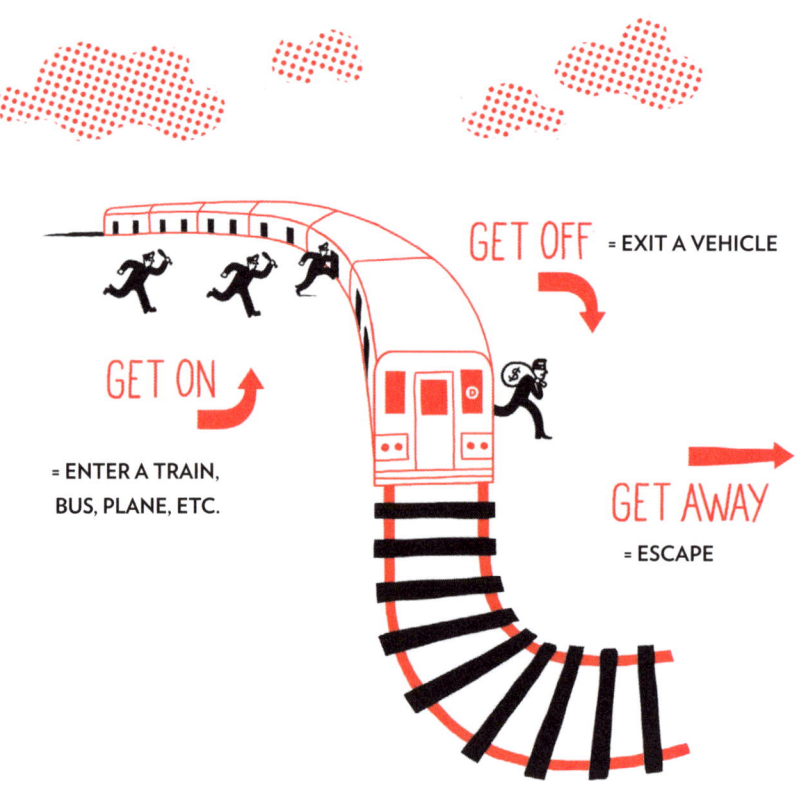

GET OFF = EXIT A VEHICLE

GET ON = ENTER A TRAIN, BUS, PLANE, ETC.

GET AWAY = ESCAPE

GET ON – GET OFF – GET AWAY

While the policemen were *getting on* the train to catch Billy Prank, he *got off*. Finally, he *got away*.

other meanings of

GET ON

= **ENTER A TRAIN, BUS, PLANE, ETC.**
= **CONTINUE DOING** sth.
= **AGE**

GET OFF

= **EXIT A VEHICLE**
= **ESCAPE PUNISHMENT**
= **FINISH, LEAVE WORK**
= **START A JOURNEY**
= **STOP TALKING ON THE PHONE**
= **HAVE AN ORGASM***

* When Patrick added the last stamp to his 33rd album of stamps, he *got off*.

GET AWAY

= **ESCAPE**
= **GO ON VACATION OR FOR A SHORT TRIP**
= **MOVE, LEAVE A PLACE**

GET OUT OF

= AVOID AN ACTIVITY YOU COMMITTED TO

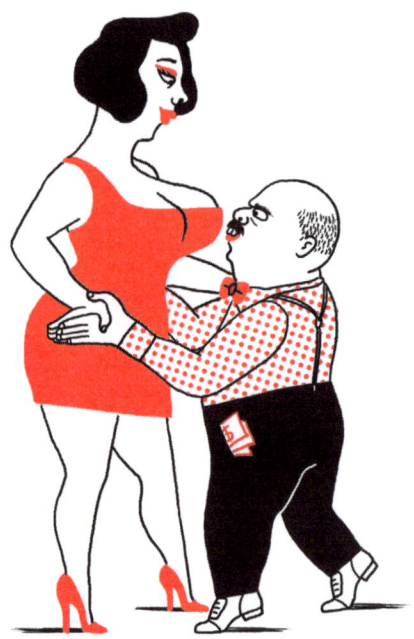

He always tries to get out of doing the cha cha cha.
But her charm prevents it.

GET something ACROSS
= GET PEOPLE TO UNDERSTAND AN IDEA

GET AHEAD
= MAKE PROGRESS

GET BY
= SURVIVE

GET OUT OF something
= LEAVE (A CAR, A TAXI, A PLACE)

GET something OUT OF something
= BENEFIT FROM

GET THROUGH (WITH)
= FINISH

GET TOGETHER (WITH SOMEONE)
= MEET UP

GET UP
= GET OUT OF BED

lesson

14

Modals
&
Similar
Expressions

Modal verbs and similar expressions:
**CAN, COULD, BE ABLE TO,
SHOULD, OUGHT TO, HAD BETTER,
HAVE TO, HAVE GOT TO, MUST,
MAY, MIGHT, WOULD, WILL.**

They are auxiliary verbs used to express
**ABILITY, ADVICE, NECESSITY,
PROHIBITION, ASSUMPTION,
FUTURE POSSIBILITY, PERMISSION,
REQUEST and SUGGESTION.**

Modals in the present are always followed by the base form of the verb
(infinitive without "to").
They have only one form, so they don't add S in the third person singular.
She <u>must</u> be lost.

BE ABLE TO, HAVE TO or **HAVE GOT TO,**
are not modals, so the conjugated form must be used!
She <u>has to</u> be lost.

CAN, COULD and BE ABLE TO
are used to express ability.
CAN'T, COULDN'T and NOT BE ABLE TO
are used to express inability.

Use CAN
for the present.

I can sing, play the guitar and ride a unicycle at the same time.
I can't teach you. I don't know how I do it.

Use COULD
for the past.

I could laugh at my classmates without regrets when I was child.
I couldn't understand English before I read this book.

Use BE ABLE TO
for all verb tenses.
"Be able to" in the present or past is more formal than "can" or "could".
With "be able to", use the correct form for each verb tense.

I'm able to follow your orders, boss.
She wasn't able to come with me.
Will you be able to go to Berlin next summer?
I like being able to do what I like.

SHOULD, OUGHT TO and **HAD BETTER**
or **SHOULDN'T, OUGHT NOT** and **HAD BETTER NOT**
are used to give advice.

SHOULD and **OUGHT TO**
mean the same thing, but *should* is more common.
They are used in the present and future tenses.
You <u>should</u> leave him.
We <u>shouldn't</u> forget they are humans.
You <u>ought to</u> just be yourself.

The negative form of *ought to* is OUGHT NOT (without "to").
She <u>ought not </u>watch this movie. She'll be afraid tonight.

SHOULD
is used to ask for advice.
<u>Should</u> I quit my job?

HAD BETTER
is used for recommendations:
You'<u>d better</u> stop smoking.
desperate hope or implied threat:
He'<u>d better not</u> be having an affair.
to warn people:
You'<u>d better not</u> run so much, this road is dangerous!

to give ADVICE

You **ought to** just be yourself.

to express NECESSITY

HAVE TO, HAVE GOT TO and MUST
are used to express obligation or necessity.

HAVE TO
is more common for general obligations.
HAVE GOT TO
expresses a stronger feeling.
"Have got to" is used in conversation and informal writing.
People <u>have to</u> pay taxes.
You<u>'ve got to</u> see this clown. He's really funny.

———————————

MUST and HAVE TO
are more common for specific and personal obligations.
"Have to" can be used in all contexts.
I <u>must</u> be on time at work, it's my first day.
I <u>have to</u> be on time at work, it's my first day.

"Must" is used in official instructions and manuals.
Employees <u>must</u> wash hands before returning to work.

———————————

"Have got to" and "must" are used in present and future tenses.
"Have to" can be used in all verb tenses.
She <u>has to</u> study a lot in order to pass the exam.
She <u>will have to</u> study a lot in order to pass the exam.

"Have to" and "must" can also be used for strong advice.
You <u>have to</u> see a shrink, you're mad!
You <u>must</u> eat more!

to express
NONNECESSITY

DON'T HAVE TO
is used to express when something
is not necessary.
It can be used for all verb tenses.
You <u>don't have to</u> do this right now.
We <u>didn't have to</u> be nice.
*I <u>won't have to</u> get up early any more
because I've been fired.*

to express
PROHIBITION

MUSTN'T
is used to express prohibition.
It can be used in present and future tenses.
You <u>mustn't</u> hit people.
You <u>mustn't</u> drive without a license.
CAN'T
is also used to express prohibition.
You <u>can't</u> drive without a license.

to express ASSUMPTIONS

MUST, HAVE TO, HAVE GOT TO, MAY, MIGHT, COULD
and CAN'T, COULDN'T, MUSTN'T, MAY NOT, MIGHT NOT
are used to express assumptions.

These modals express certainty or doubt.
They are used in the present.

MUST, HAVE TO and HAVE GOT TO
express 100% affirmative certainty.
MAY, MIGHT and COULD
express less certainty.

CAN'T and COULDN'T
express 100% negative certainty.
MUSTN'T
expresses slightly less negative certainty.
MAY NOT and MIGHT NOT
express even less negative certainty.

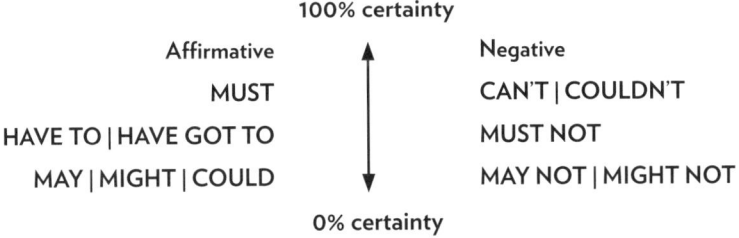

	100% certainty	
Affirmative	↑	Negative
MUST		CAN'T | COULDN'T
HAVE TO | HAVE GOT TO		MUST NOT
MAY | MIGHT | COULD	↓	MAY NOT | MIGHT NOT
	0% certainty	

to talk about

FUTURE POSSIBILITY

MAY, MIGHT and **COULD**
are used to express possibility.

MAY, MIGHT and **COULD** are the same.
The store may open at 10 tomorrow.
The store might open at 10 tomorrow.
The store could open at 10 tomorrow.

MAY NOT and **MIGHT NOT**
express the possibility that something will not happen.
The store may not open at 10.
The store might not open at 10.

"May" and "might" aren't usually used in questions about possiblities.
Other forms are used:
Will the store open at 10?
Do you think the store will be open at 10?

to ask PERMISSION

MAY and **CAN**
are used to ask permission.

MAY is more formal.
May I smoke here?
No, but you may smoke outside.
CAN is more informal.
Can I smoke here, buddy?
You can smoke outside, my dear.

to make
REQUESTS

WOULD, COULD, WILL and **CAN**
are used to make requests.

WOULD and **COULD** are more formal.
Would you please bring me a coffee?
Could you do my homework?
WILL or **CAN** are used informally in speech.
Will you tell me a story?
Can you leave me alone?

to offer
SUGGESTIONS

WOULD YOU LIKE, SHALL and **SHOULD**
are used to offer and suggest.
"Shall" is only used in the first person singular and plural.
Would you like a beer?
Shall we take a walk?
Should we go out tonight?

For informal situations:
LET'S, WHY DON'T WE and HOW ABOUT.
Let's take a walk!
Why don't we go out?
How about getting something to drink?

QUESTiON
TaGs

Question tags are short questions at the end of a sentence.
They are used for confirmation.
It's a beautiful day, isn't it?
And to ask for information or help.
You don't know where the station is, do you?

They are composed of:
AUXILIARY VERB + SUBJECT
of the sentence.

For a positive sentence, use a negative tag.
She dances very well, <u>doesn't she?</u>
You're tired, <u>aren't you?</u>

For a negative sentence, use a positive tag.
You don't like me, <u>do you?</u>

Imperative question tags usually use "will".
Shut up, <u>will you?</u>

lesson

Conditionals describe situations and circumstances that entail cause and effect.
If a particular condition is present, a particular result occurs.

Conditionals are composed of two clauses:
the **IF CLAUSE** and the **RESULT CLAUSE**.

You can begin conditional sentences
with the "if clause" or the result clause.
The meaning is the same.

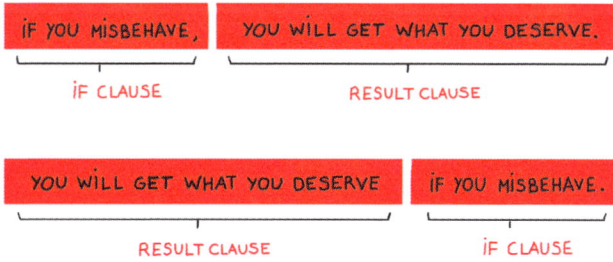

Note that if the "if clause" comes first,
a **COMMA** is used between the two clauses.

ZERO CONDITIONAL

IF + SIMPLE PRESENT... , ... SIMPLE PRESENT...
If you heat water to 100 degrees, it boils.

IF YOU HEAT WATER TO 100 DEGREES CELSIUS, IT BOILS.

For **GENERAL TRUTHS**.

You can often use "when" instead of "if".
<u>When</u> you heat water to 100 degrees celsius, it boils.

If Susan feels inspired, she sings.

For **HABITS**
and things that always happen.

You can use
simple present or present continuous
in the "if clause".

**IF + PRESENT CONTINUOUS... ,
... SIMPLE PRESENT...**
If Susan _is feeling_ happy, she _dances._

To give **INSTRUCTIONS**
or **INVITATIONS**
dependent on certain conditions,
use the imperative with the "if clause".

**IF ... PRESENT SIMPLE... ,
... IMPERATIVE ...**
If you _are_ free, _come_ over for dinner.

Come over for dinner if you are free.

FIRST CONDITIONAL

IF + SIMPLE PRESENT... , ... FUTURE SIMPLE...
If you love me, you will stay with me.

First conditional is used to talk about **FUTURE POSSIBILITIES**.

Instead of simple present, you can also use other present tenses:
PRESENT CONTINUOUS: *If you <u>are feeling</u> bored, I'll sing you a song.*
PRESENT PERFECT SIMPLE: *If you <u>have</u> already <u>eaten</u> chicken today,*
I'll give you chicken tomorrow.
PRESENT PERFECT CONTINUOUS: *If you <u>have been watching</u> TV, I'll throw it away.*

IF SHE GETS DISTRACTED, I CAN ESCAPE.

UNLESS HE SUDDENLY LEAVES, I WILL BE ABLE TO ESCAPE UNNOTICED.

WILL is a modal verb. Other **MODAL VERBS**
express different meanings.
If she gets distracted, I _can_ escape | I _could_ escape | I _might_ be able to escape.

IF can be replaced with:
WHETHER: *Whether he suddenly leaves or not, I'll be able to escape unnoticed.*
(=if he leaves and if he doesn't)
UNLESS: *Unless he suddenly leaves, I'll be able to escape unnoticed.* (=if he doesn't leave)

SECOND CONDITIONAL

IF + SIMPLE PAST... , ... WOULD + VERB (infinitive without "to") ...
If men liked her, she would be happy.

Second conditional is used to talk about **HYPOTHETICAL SITUATIONS**.

Hypothetical situations are:

IMAGINARY SITUATIONS

If I were married, I would make my husband the happiest man in the world.

IMPOSSIBLE

If I were a man, I would like hairy women.

IMPROBABLE

If I had a lover, I would tickle him with my hair.

In addition to the simple past, you can use:
PAST CONTINUOUS: *If you <u>were looking</u> for a lover, I might be available.*

In addition to "would", you can use:
COULD: *If I were wealthy, I <u>could</u> buy everything I need.*
MIGHT: *If I shaved off my beard, I <u>might</u> be able to get married.*

THIRD CONDITIONAL

IF + PAST PERFECT... , ... WOULD HAVE + PAST PARTICIPLE...
If I had lived longer, I would have loved much more.

Third conditional is used to talk about **PAST HYPOTHETICAL SITUATIONS**,
things that didn't happen in the past.

In addition to "would have", you can use:

SHOULD HAVE: *If he had hurt your feelings, he <u>should have</u> apologized.*

COULD HAVE: *If I had realized it sooner, I <u>could have</u> gotten together with the woman who brings me flowers.*

MIGHT HAVE: *If I I had been luckier, I <u>might have</u> succeeded in life.*

If or Whether?

"If" and "whether" are similar, but there are some differences.

Use **IF**:
To express a condition.
In conditional sentences, "if" introduces the condition.
If something annoys you, look for a solution.

Use **WHETHER**:
To present two alternatives.
I wonder whether I should have added a little more poison to his tea.
(=Should I have added more poison or not?)

After prepositions.
We argued about whether I behaved rudely towards him.

Before infinitives.
I've been thinking about whether to get rid of everything that annoys me.

Use **WHETHER** or **IF**:
Reporting yes | no questions.
She wondered whether | if he was right.
The question is: *Was he right?*

In WHETHER | IF... OR... constructions.
I would like to know whether | if the problem is me or him.

lesson 16

IDioMS

Idioms are
EXPRESSIONS
with a meaning that is not literal.
They don't always follow the usual
language pattern.

It's Raining Cats and Dogs

= it's raining very heavily.

Hit The Sack

= go to bed.

HAVE A FROG IN ONE'S THROAT

= have a feeling of losing one's voice, usually out of fear.

BE BENT OUT OF SHAPE

= be upset, angry, offended.

BARK UP THE WRONG TREE

= go to the wrong person or place for something.

MAKE ENDS MEET

= have enough money to cover expenses.

LAUGH ALL THE WAY TO THE BANK

= be happy for having made money, usually because of sth. ridiculed or thought worthless.

BE ON THE EDGE OF ONE'S SEAT

= enthusiastically watch a performance.

HAVE A SEAT

= sit down.

DO YOUR BEST

= do something as well as you can.

DON'T GIVE ME ANY LIP!

= don't talk back!

MONKEY SEE,

MONKEY DO

= imitate in a mindless, automatic way.

COUNT ON SOMEONE
= rely on someone.

BE ON THE FENCE
= be undecided.

STEW IN ONE'S OWN JUICES
= be left alone to suffer one's anger.

GET ONE'S FOOT IN THE DOOR
= have an opportunity.

BE UNDER THE WEATHER
= be ill.

DROP A HINT
= give an indirect suggestion.

SWEAT BULLETS
= be very anxious.

IN GOOD SHAPE
= in good physical condition.

WITH BELLS ON
= eagerly and on time.

Look Like a Million Dollars

= look great, extremely attractive.

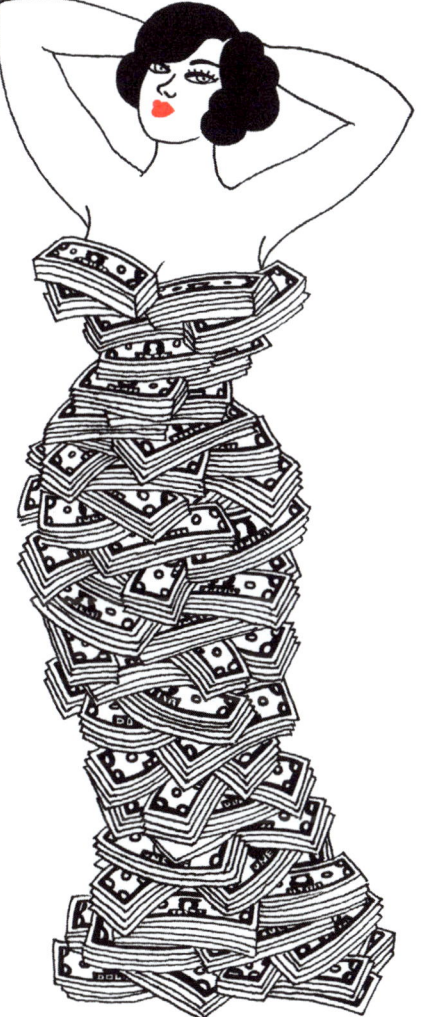

TaLK CRaP

or TALK SHIT = insult someone
or lie, or both at the same time.

Be MiLeS AwaY

= be totally distracted.

Be ALL EaRS

= pay close attention.

HANG IN THERE
= persist despite difficulties.

EVERY CLOUD HAS A SILVER LINING
= bad things result in something good.

HAVE A BLAST
= have a great time.

TIT FOR TAT
AN EYE FOR AN EYE | A TOOTH FOR A TOOTH
= take revenge by repeating the same offense.

BE GREEN WITH ENVY
= be very jealous of what someone else has.

SHAKE IN ONE'S SHOES
= be very frightened or anxious.

HIT THE BULL'S-EYE
= achieve something precise.

GET OFF ON THE WRONG FOOT
= start something badly.

ONE'S CUP OF TEA
= something one prefers, likes.

RACE AGAINST THE CLOCK
= do something quickly because of a pressing deadline.

JOG SOMEONE'S MEMORY
= stimulate so. to remember something.

MONEY TALKS
= money has power and influence.

DRIVE SOMEONE TO DISTRACTION
= confuse or perplex someone.

HAVE BUTTERFLIES IN ONE'S STOMACH
= be very nervous.

CATCH RED-HANDED
= catch so. in the act of doing something bad.

GO NUTS | GO BANANAS
= go crazy.

MAKE UP ONE'S MIND
= decide something.

KEEP ONE'S CHIN UP
= be positive.

WHEN PIGS FLY
WHEN HELL FREEZES OVER
= never.

Live on The Edge

= live dangerously.

Like
Two Peas in a Pod

= very similar.

CRY OVER SPILT MILK

= be unhappy about what can't be undone.

KEEP ONE'S EYE ON THE BALL

= to remain alert to what is happening around you.

CHANGE ONE'S MIND

= change ideas or opinions.

MY LIPS ARE SEALED

= I will keep a secret.

BEAT ONESELF UP

= punish oneself over past actions.

CUT CORNERS

= do a job quickly, sloppily.

(I, you, he...) CAN'T STAND

= (I, you, he...) extremely dislike.

GET INTO A JAM

= get into a bad situation.

GET OUT OF A JAM

= find a solution to a problem or a bad situation.

NOT SLEEP A WINK

= not sleep at all.

SLEEP LIKE A LOG

= sleep very well, deeply.

WORK LIKE A DOG

= work very hard.

HIT THE ROAD

= go away.

BREAK A LEG!

= good luck!

GIVE SOMEBODY THE EVIL EYE

= look at so. in a way thought to bring them misfortune or bad luck.

SMELL A RAT

= sense that something is wrong.

BE IN HOT WATER

= be in trouble.

A DIME A DOZEN

= very common, easy to find.

YOU BET!

= yes! | you're welcome!

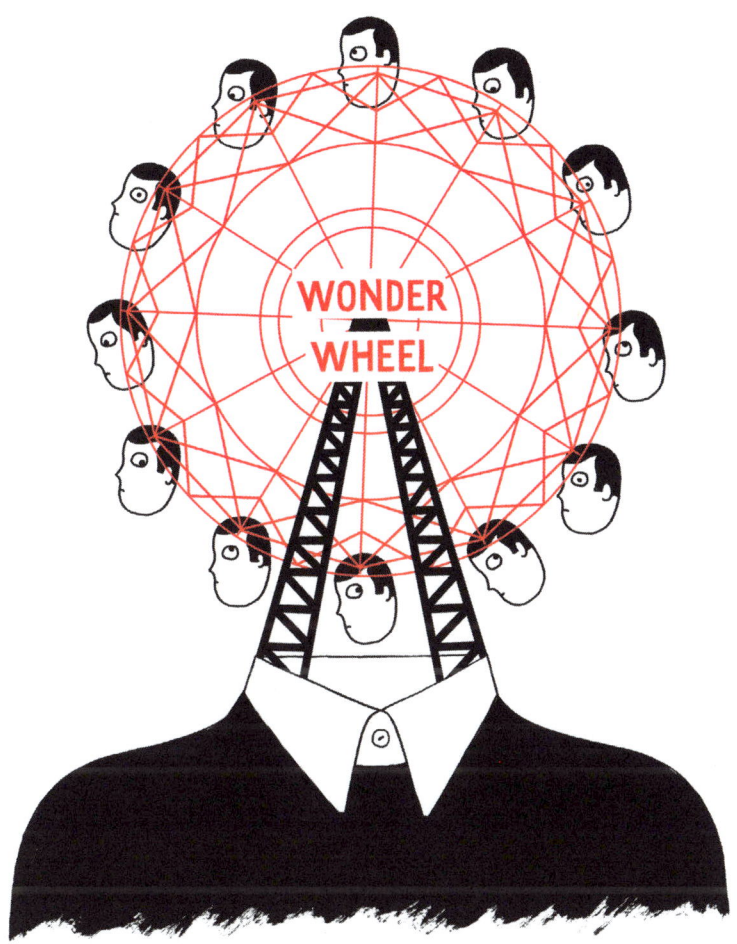

MY HeaD iS SpinNiNG

= I have too many decisions to make
or too many things to think about.

lesson

17

USEFUL

EXPRESSIONS

Vocabulary you need to survive.

To ask for forgiveness.

When someone sneezes.

A common toast before clinking glasses.

To tell someone to be attentive to possible danger.

To insist that someone do something faster.

When you first meet someone.

To get someone's attention.

To have someone repeat something.

INSULTS

Offensive words used towards others.

= an unintelligent person.

Imbecile

Motherfucker

= a very despicable person.

Asshole

= an obnoxious, arrogant, rude, irritating person.

Asskisser

also ASSLICKER
= a person who
will do anything
to be liked.

Bitch

= a malicious
or unpleasant
woman.

Fuck off

= go away.

CONNECTED SPEECH

When two words are pronounced as one
in speech and informal writing.

My mother's **gonna** drive me crazy.

= GOING TO

You **gotta** be careful with me.

= HAVE GOT TO

I **wanna** kiss you.

= WANT TO

We **woulda** won if they hadn't.

= WOULD HAVE

It **coulda** been worse.

= COULD HAVE

She **shoulda** waxed her moustache.

= SHOULD HAVE

ACRONYMS

A word formed from the initial letters of a group of words.
They are very common in written and spoken English.

Common acronyms:

TGIF
Thank God It's Friday

ASAP
As Soon As Possible

FYI
For Your Information

LOL
Laughing Out Loud

AKA
Also Known As

ID
Identification

BTW
By The Way

XOXO
Hugs And Kissess

FAQs
Frequently Asked Questions

RIP
Rest In Peace

index

SIORI MASA ENRIQUE ME JON NICHOLAS ? MARC ROBERT

acknowledgements

Thanks to the thief who stole my purse and sketchbook, where
most of these drawings come from, and who then threw the
sketchbook in the trash for me to find later.

Thanks to the people in the picture, who were all with me
during that special time in New York.
And thanks to Arnal, who is still with me.